Dating, Mating and Relating

Inspiring, informative books for thoughtful readers wanting to make changes and realise their potential.

Other **titles in the series** include:

Choosing a Better Life
An inspiring step-by-step guide to
building the future you want

Building Your Life Skills
Who are you, where are you, and where do you want to go: a personal action plan

When What You've Got Is Not What You Want
Use NLP to create the life you want
and live it to the full

Living the Life You Want
Your personal key to true abundance and richness of everyday experience

Please send for a free copy of the catalogue for full details
(see back cover for address).

Dating, Mating and Relating

The complete guide to finding and keeping your ideal partner

Susan Nash

PATHWAYS

First published in 2000 by
How To Books Ltd., 3 Newtec Place,
Magdalen Road, Oxford OX4 1RE, United Kingdom
Tel: 01865 793806   Fax: 01865 248780

British Library Cataloguing in Publication Data
A catalogue record for this book is available from
the British Library

Edited by Diana Brueton   Cover image PhotoDisc
Cover design by Shireen Nathoo Design
Cover copy by Sallyann Sheridan

Produced for How To Books by Deer Park Productions
Typeset by Anneset, Weston-super-Mare, Somerset
Printed and bound in Great Britain

Note: The material contained in this book is set out in good
faith for general guidance and no liability can be accepted for loss or expense
incurred as a result of relying in particular circumstances on statements made in
the book. The laws and regulations are complex and liable to change, and readers
should check the current position with the relevant authorities before making
personal arrangements.

Pathways is an imprint of
How To Books

Contents

List of Illustrations   ix

Introduction   xi

1.   **Defining lovemates**   1
    Understanding ourselves   1
    Defining temperament   2
    Origins of temperament   3
    Self-assessment   5
    Descriptions of temperaments   8
    You can't escape who you are   16
    Case studies   16
    Discussion points   18
    Summary   19

2   **Loving in your own style**   20
    From lovemates to loving styles   20
    Understanding functions   21
    Discovering your functions   23
    Information-gathering functions   24
    Delving deeper into information-gathering   26
    Decision-making approaches   29
    Delving deeper into decision-making functions   31
    Direction of energy   35
    Tying it all together   37
    Loving styles and relationships   41
    Case studies   41
    Discussion points   43
    Summary   43

3   **Valuing differences**   45
    Nature or nurture?   45
    Identifying life events   48
    Understanding male/female differences   49

Identifying personality differences   51
The battle of the temperaments   55
Functions and differences   59
Mapping your relationship   65
Celebrating the unique quality of your relationship   67
Case studies   68
Discussion points   74
Summary   74

4   **Managing the dating game**   76
Understanding the dating stage   76
Factors of attraction   77
Defining the signs and the signals   80
Understanding the stages of the game   82
The playing field   84
Lovemates and dating   85
Functions and dating   88
Case studies   91
Discussion points   95
Summary   95

5   **Building a foundation in the mating stage**   97
Defining the mating stage   97
Writing a vision statement   99
Defining joint goals   101
Establishing your values and guiding principles   105
Managing reality   108
Lovemates and loving styles in the mating stage   110
Case studies   114
Discussion points   119
Summary   120

6   **Relating: communicating with your mate**   121
Defining the relating stage   121
Communicating   121
What is communication?   122
Building the communication process   123
Complexity of the process   124
Sending the message   125

Obtaining a response   132
Adapting your style   133
Providing positive feedback   140
Case study   143
Discussion points   145
Summary   146

7   **Relating: dealing with conflicts**   **148**
Defining conflict   148
Recognizing sources of conflict   148
Understanding your response to conflict   150
Communicating assertively   150
Managing conflict situations   153
Making decisions   160
Loving styles and conflict   163
Case study   166
Discussion points   169
Summary   169

8   **Relating: spending quality time together**   **171**
The pressure of time   171
Prioritizing work/life balance   174
Understanding leisure time   177
Understanding gender differences   181
Spending holidays together   183
Case studies   184
Discussion points   187
Summary   188

Summary: keeping the passion alive   **190**

Appendix   **191**
Further reading   **205**
Index   **207**

List of Illustrations

1	Conscious/unconscious – competence/incompetence	2
2	Functions and organising a wedding	23
3	To focus: the seven lenses of personality	46
4	To focus, focused	47
5	Sample lifeline	49
6	Sample lifeline	69
7	The four supports of the partnership	98
8	Sample vision statement	100
9	Sample vision statement and logo	116
10	Sample vision statement and logo	117
11	The communication process	123
12	Reasoning an emotions graph	154
13	Prioritizing work/life	175
14	Venn diagram	182
15	Sample Venn diagram: Andrew and Christine	186

Anyone can be with anyone if both parties work to understand and value their differences

Dating, Mating and Relating

> *You've been in a relationship for several years. You thought she was 'the one'. Now you feel the flame is starting to flicker; the two of you are arguing more, and you're wondering if you made a mistake. Why?*

Many of our underlying beliefs around relationships are largely based on the idea that there is a perfect mate for us, with whom we will live our lives 'happily ever after'. So who is this elusive someone?

In the hundreds of training programmes I have run on type and temperament, the one question I hear without fail is, 'Based on personality type, who should I be with?' The good news is, while many of society's communication vehicles infer there is a perfect mate for every person, our premise in *Dating, Mating, and Relating* is that *anyone can be with anyone . . .*' if both parties respect, understand, and celebrate the differences between them and are committed to making the relationship work.

However, many of us are looking for a simple answer or a 'quick fix' in resolving partnership differences. When we told people we were writing this book, they nearly lined up for advance purchases. People are intrigued by anything that shows the slightest possibility of helping them to develop successful intimate relationships. If you consider the huge divorce rates in western society it is easy to understand the appeal.

In reality, sustainable long-term relationships and quick fixes are mutually exclusive. However most couples, if they understand each other better, comprehend the different steps in relationships and are both willing to put in the hard work necessary, can create a successful partnership.

> 'Keeping the relationship intact is at the heart of our actions, choices and decisions.'
>
> *On Commitment*

Defining the steps in a relationship

Three main stages have been identified in intimate relationships: lust, or what we call the **dating stage**, limerance, or the **mating stage**, and attachment, the **relating stage**.

- The dating stage can last for up to six months, depending on the pace a couple moves, and is characterised by extreme sexual attraction.

- The mating stage can last from six months to four years and is characterised by intense absorption in the other person, almost to the exclusion of anything else. This is the feeling most of us associate with 'being in love'.

- There are no estimates on the length of time the relating stage can last, but ideally it should see out the lifetime of the couple. It is characterised by commitment, sharing and a deep friendship: the feeling most of us associate with 'loving', but without all the intense highs and lows of the 'in love' phase.

Moving from the mating to the relating stage proves to be the biggest challenge in our consumer, 'chuck it in and buy a new one' society. A change in the level of excitement, the presence of fights or issues, etc are often interpreted as meaning the relationship has lost its passion and is not meant to be. So it is concluded that we should continue looking for the right person. Instead this is a natural phase in the development of a successful relationship.

> 'I made a commitment to her that I would make this work, and to take the good with the complex.'
>
> *On Commitment*

What is the purpose of this book?

This book will not tell you what is wrong with you, but what is right with you! By understanding how to make what is right with you work with what is right with your partner, you can circumvent the divorce statistics. This book provides an objective framework for understanding and working with those differences.

Using this book

In this book we provide information and an approach to building an effective long-term partnership, using specific exercises within each section.

However, you cannot just read this book and practise the techniques on your partner. A relationship cannot be a one-way effort and neither is this book. *Dating, Mating, and Relating* is an interactive approach to relationships; you must both review the material and complete the exercises together to really benefit from the methodology.

In Chapters 1 and 2 we focus on helping you to better understand yourself, and what is important to you. If we don't know, like and understand ourselves, how can we hope to understand our partner? We will profile individual personality by identifying lovemates and then loving styles.

In Chapter 3 we focus on profiling your current partnership, if you are in one. We will identify the inherent connections between you (the things that probably attracted you to each other in the first place) and the source of potential conflicts (those things that probably drive you mad about your partner). Then, depending on the stage you are currently experiencing in your relationship, you can choose from the following chapters based on what is the most relevant to you.

In Chapter 4 you will learn about the factors that attract you to another, but which might not necessarily provide the grounding for a positive relationship. We also describe the dating rituals and show you how to stop playing the dating game, and find a person who is right for you.

In Chapter 5 you will learn how to lay the foundation in the mating stage: the stage most often associated with being passionately in love, as well as most accepting of differences, which makes it the ideal time to agree on goals and interactive approaches.

In Chapters 6 to 8 you will be given information and techniques to enable you to build a successful long-term partnership in the relating phase.

Each chapter includes examples, exercises, case studies, and discussion points, so that you can directly apply the principles introduced with your partner to help improve your relationship and keep the passion alive. The good news is that your chances of sustaining a long-term relationship are not 50/50. They are what you make of them. Just remember the following guidelines:

- Building relationships takes commitment from both parties.
- Understanding the differences between you can be a tool in this process.
- Making a relationship successful is hard work – sorry, no quick fixes here!
- The benefits to adopting this approach are well worth the costs.

> 'Coming together is a beginning: keeping together is progress: Working together is success.'
>
> *Henry Ford*

Reading this book is taking a proactive and positive step toward success. Good luck!

CHAPTER 1

Defining lovemates

While most of us have lived with ourselves a long time, many of us do not necessarily understand what makes us tick. The first step in improving your relationships is to better understand what is important to you, and how you approach the situations in your life. To do this we will introduce you to the theory of temperament: four broad patterns of personality, which have been identified and described for over 25 centuries. In relationships we call these four temperaments lovemates. Discovering the type of lovemate you are will help you to better know yourself and relate to others.

Understanding ourselves

When I raised the topic of self-knowledge, while working with a 50 year-old client from IBM, his reply was, 'Do you honestly think people reach the age of 50 without knowing themselves?' Absolutely. Understanding what is important to us, and how we operate is not necessarily as obvious as you might think.

> 'The unexamined life is not worth living.'
>
> *Socrates*

Looking inside ourselves and trying to sort out the collage of abilities, skills, strengths, and weaknesses that make up our personality can be quite a challenge. While we are aware of certain talents, we all have areas in which we are completely oblivious to our strengths (unconscious competence) or worse, our weaknesses (unconscious incompetence).

The grid on the next page (Figure 1) is a useful model in this process of self-discovery.

The implications of this possible lack of self-knowledge on

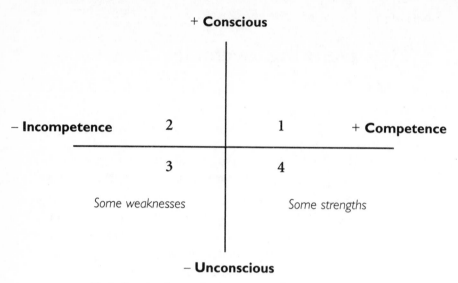

Fig. 1. Conscious/unconscious – competence/incompetence.

partnerships are considerable. If you have this innate talent you might become frustrated with your partner, because they do not behave this way. In contrast if this is an unconscious area of weakness for you, you might expect your partner to 'step into the gap' and he or she might be unable to do so. Plus, if you both possess a certain talent, it can prove an important point of connection between the two of you.

Understanding how we are 'hard-wired' can shortcut the process of self-knowledge, and provide an objective framework for comprehending the differing strengths and weaknesses we each possess. When we look at temperament, and later at loving style, you will find that you each have characteristics that fall into all four quadrants. By striving to understand these areas, we broaden our perspective and ability to relate to each other.

Defining temperament

As human beings we are all unique individuals. Our genetics coupled with our background, culture, education and life experiences intermingle to create our individual character. Even identical twins are each unique. However, four underlying personality patterns have been consistently and cross-culturally recognized for over 25 centuries. We call these personality themes

temperaments. Our temperament is based on a set of core needs and values that drive our behaviour. These driving forces are the essence of our being; they permeate our likes, dislikes, talents, behaviours, approaches and paradigms.

This is not to say that if people have the same temperament they are identical. They will share core needs and show similarities in behaviour, but they will probably look very different, as the template of their shared temperament will be coloured by their own unique experiences.

> 'Our knowledge is a little island in a great ocean of non-knowledge.'
> *On Not Labelling*, Henry Kaiser

Origins of temperament

Scholars have observed and written about these four distinct patterns of personality since nearly the beginning of recorded time. As far back as 450 BC the Greek physician and father of medicine, Hippocrates, described four types of people based on the predominance of one of the body 'humours' (fluids). He described the sanguine as excited and impulsive, the melancholic as morose and serious, the phlegmatic as calm or impassive and the choleric as sensitive and emotional. In the Middle Ages another physician responsible for the application of chemistry to medicine, Paracelsus, recognized four 'natures' found in humans along the same four themes of Hippocrates' work. Four different spirits of nature guided his four dispositions: the salamander spirit of fire, the gnome of the earth, the sylph of the air and the nymph spirit of water. In America the medicine wheel of the American Plains Indians also recognized four similar personality themes. Each individual was born into one of four perceptions: the bear way of connecting to the environment, the mouse way of staying grounded and close to the roots of life, the buffalo way of logic and analysis and the eagle way of seeing patterns and floating above the details. In the early 20th century psychologists such as Eric Adickes, Ernst Kretchemer and Eduard Spranger also recognized these four types based on corresponding personality traits.

Keirsey's contribution

David Keirsey, a behavioural scientist, developed the modern theory of temperament in 1956. Keirsey was impressed by the consistencies in temperament portraits throughout history and spent over 40 years researching and integrating the descriptions into a comprehensive systems theory of temperament. He referred to the four temperaments as **artisans, guardians, rationals** and **idealists**. In relationships, Keirsey provided the following names for each temperament, which we refer to as **lovemates** throughout the remainder of the book:

◆ artisan = playmate
◆ guardian = helpmate
◆ rational = mindmate
◆ idealist = soulmate.

Let's look at each of the four lovemates in more detail.

◆ Playmates live one day at a time, seizing the day and all the freedom they can get. They are alert to opportunities, respond to the needs of the situation, and need to make an impact in their environment.

> 'The right man is the one who seizes the moment.'
> *Johann Wolfgang Von Goethe*

◆ Helpmates are driven by responsibility and duty, wishing to serve and protect those they care about. They are the pillars of society, stable and supportive, yet they also need membership and belonging within a group.

> 'There are two ways of spreading light: to be the candle or the mirror that receives it.'
> *Emily Wharton*

◆ Mindmates seek knowledge and competence in all they take on. They seek to understand the operating principles of all around them and create their own destiny.

> 'I don't think much of a man who is not wiser today than he was yesterday.'
> *Abraham Lincoln*

◆ Soulmates are soul-searchers who constantly quest for meaning and significance in their lives. They want to make a difference and are constantly on a journey to find and be their unique self and help others do the same.

> 'Happiness is when what you think, and what you say and what you do are in harmony.'
>
> *Mahatma Gandi*

Self-assessment

Before detailed descriptions are given of each of the four lovemates, let's stop and think about you.

What do you bring to a relationship?

(a) What strengths do you feel you bring to a relationship? Think about relationships you've been in and your strengths in general. It could be you lighten things up with your sense of humour, or maybe your date planning prowess keeps the adventure alive.

(b) Then there is the 'baggage' that you bring to a relationship – your weaknesses. What have partners told you that you needed to work on? What behaviours did you demonstrate that caused problems in previous relationships?

Make lists of (a) strengths in a relationship and (b) weaknesses in a relationship. We will return to these lists after a brief discussion of the four lovemates.

Quick temperament sorter

Currently, no accurate assessment for temperament exists. This quick sorter is designed to help indicate which lovemate(s) you should consider.

(a) Read the word choices in the left column.

(b) Choose the response that is most like you, *not* the one you want to be like.

(c) Rank the choices in each row from 1 to 4, 1 being the most like you, 4 being the least like you.

	1	2	3	4
Need. . .	To make a difference	Self-control and competence	To be part of a group/family	Freedom to make things happen
Value. . .	Uniqueness and meaning	Expertise and mastery	Responsibility and duty	Excitement and adventure
Enjoy. . .	Growth and development	Theory and debate	Nuturing and being needed	Making an impression
Descriptive verb. . .	Becoming	Knowing	Protecting	Doing
In setting a direction, need a. . .	Meaningful purpose	Strategy	Step-by-step approach	Action plan/goal
In relationships need. . .	Inner exploration	Autonomy and respect of ideas	Security	Excitement
Like feedback that is. . .	Genuine and specific	Recognizing intelligence and ideas	Constructive and specific	Frequent and direct
Words are. . .	Dramatic and flowing	Precise and elaborate	Specific and clear	Colloquial and to the point
Admire. . .	Realized potential	Knowledge and design	Achievement	Skill and beauty
Seek in life. . .	Meaning	Knowledge	Membership	Opportunity
Would hate to be. . .	Average	Incompetent	Excluded	Confined
Ideal relationship	Expressive and mystic	Innovative and intellectual	Organized and secure	Stimulating and varied
Core abilities	Diplomacy/ building bridges	Developing strategies/ analyzing frameworks	Logistics/ operations	Tactics/ performance with skill
Relationship motto	'Love conquers all.'	'Love and respect as equals.'	'Home is where the heart is'	'Love like you're never gonna get hurt. . .'
TOTAL				

(d) After answering all the questions, total each column in the boxes provided. Each column is an indicator of the following temperament:

Column 1 = soulmate
Column 2 = mindmate
Column 3 = helpmate
Column 4 = playmate

Review the matrix and descriptions for each temperament that follows, looking for which one seems most like you.

Strengths and possible weaknesses in a relationship

Now let's review the 'typical' answers from each lovemate for the strengths and possible weakness in a relationship.

Temperament	Strengths	Possible weaknesses
Playmate	◆ Bring a sense of excitement ◆ Stimulate a variety of experiences ◆ Allow their partner freedom ◆ Help partner to live more in the moment	◆ May have trouble committing ◆ May get bored easily and appear frivolous ◆ May want to have fun all the time ◆ May not plan ahead
Helpmate	◆ Loyal to relationships ◆ Live up to responsibilities and promises ◆ Are respectful of partner ◆ Organize time together, to get the most out of it	◆ Can be too structured ◆ May have trouble making changes ◆ Can appear to nag at 'irresponsible' partners ◆ May not stand up for their own needs
Mindmate	◆ Bring an abstract future focused perspective ◆ Use a logical perspective when problem-solving ◆ Tend to be independent minded ◆ Will generate ideas	◆ May appear oblivious to feelings ◆ Can be too intense May enjoy working too much ◆ May appear that they won't open up and are cold
Soulmate	◆ Desire to help the partner grow and achieve ◆ Ability to help partner open up; create intimacy ◆ Facilitate meaningful discussions ◆ Recognition of uniqueness and the 'real person'	◆ Can be overly emotional with constant crises ◆ May avoid conflict or lash out ◆ May need constant positive reinforcement ◆ Can read too much into things

Descriptions of temperaments

As you look through the matrix and descriptions remember that temperament is a pattern, not a set of definitive characteristics. There will be aspects of each lovemate that you see in yourself. However, one lovemate will be your best fit. It is this best fit temperament that really describes our underlying core needs and values, whether you are aware of them or not.

Temperament	What's important	How they act
Playmate	◆ Acting in the moment and making an impact ◆ Freedom to do what they want ◆ Variety ◆ Aesthetic appeal ◆ Physical adeptness ◆ Skilled performance ◆ Cool tools and resources ◆ Seeing the immediate concrete results ◆ Present focus. Life is an adventure	◆ Quick-moving and physically expressive ◆ Restless and spontaneous ◆ Talk in colloquialisms ◆ Take risks ◆ Seize opportunities ◆ Tell great stories ◆ May use concrete physical humour ◆ 'Net it out' in communication: 'What's the bottom line?'
Helpmate	◆ Being part of a team or family ◆ Living up to responsibilities ◆ Designated roles (hierarchy) and duties ◆ Security and stability ◆ Having a structured approach to situations and activities ◆ Seeing a concrete achievement ◆ Being economical with resources whether time, money, etc ◆ Abiding by rules and regulations ◆ Past focus: life is a process	◆ More deliberate, conservative body language ◆ Talk about past experience ◆ Use the language of the group ◆ Skilled in logistics ◆ Are reliable ◆ Will begin at the beginning and move step-by-step through a discussion ◆ May use dry, tongue-in-cheek humour ◆ Will want to provide all the details when communicating

Temperament	Whats important	How they act
Mindmate	◆ Intelligence and competence in what they do ◆ Autonomy and shaping their own destiny ◆ Innovation and progress ◆ Designing efficiency into systems ◆ High standards for themselves and others ◆ Independent thinking ◆ Logical analysis and consistency ◆ Developing strategies ◆ Future focus: life is progress	◆ May appear arrogant or 'distant' ◆ Talk about concepts and theories ◆ Seek reason and rationale ◆ Engage in critical questioning (which can be viewed as criticism) ◆ May use word play/puns; a very cerebral humour ◆ May debate for fun ◆ Seek eloquence and preciseness in word choice: may correct word choice ◆ Seek to understand the world around them
Soulmate	◆ Being able to constantly develop their own and other people's potential ◆ Having a meaningful purpose or a cause as a focus for life's activities ◆ Being surrounded by people with whom there is a connection ◆ Diplomacy and positive interaction ◆ Being valued for their own unique contribution ◆ Authenticity ◆ Unlimited imagination ◆ Ethics ◆ Future focus: life is a journey	◆ May appear warm and welcoming using expressive gestures ◆ Show empathy and concern ◆ Talk about possibilities and ideas relating to people ◆ Language may be full of generalizations, impressions and hyperbole ◆ Humour may be self-deprecating and relevant to the person ◆ Will use supportive listening and questioning to draw out others ◆ Seek to understand the people around them

Try it now: **Temperament self-assessment**

Based on the previous information, do the following steps:

1. Look over your thoughts around your strengths and weaknesses in a relationship. Compare it to the typical answers on page 65 and note which lovemate you believe is the closest fit.

2. Review the quick temperament sorter on page 66 and note the lovemate it indicated.

3. Looking at the table on the previous page, choose the lovemate that seems most like you.

4. Review the descriptions for the lovemate(s) that you identified most with throughout these exercises. Feel free to try on multiple descriptions until you are comfortable with the one that feels like the 'best fit.'

5. Read the other lovemate decriptions to increase your awareness of how those with other temperaments view the world. As you read the other descriptions, start to think of your partner (if you are currently in a relationship) and which description appears most like him or her.

6. If possible, read the descriptions with your partner so that they can help you, and you them, in this self-selection process.

Playmates

You feel all the rounds, the smooths, the sharp edges, the flats and hollows, the lights and shades, the cools and warms. The colours and the textures. There's hundreds of little differences and all fitting together.

Joyce Cary

Playmates look for a friend and lover to share the joys of life. To the playmate life is a party and a mate is a date. Playmates usually thrive in the dating scene with its infinite variety and sensory appeal. They have a tendency to play the field, enjoying the differences in each of their love interests. In fact, their adaptability makes them the perfect match for the mate of the moment. Playmates throw themselves into their partner's interests and flex to their needs, until they grow bored and move on to something new. They may find it difficult to settle down as something else always looks more exciting and they hate confinement. However, even the master player will eventually tire of the dating game and move on to try a hand at the challenges of commitment.

Playmates are fun and exciting mates. They live for the moment, riding the tides and allowing their impulses to float them along. Playmates manoeuvre tactically from situation to situation. They are great firefighters, solving problems effectively in moments of crisis. Their mates are often in for a wild ride, unbridled by convention or fear. They are usually pushing for their mate to loosen up and have more fun. However, living to the hilt often leaves them in states of feast or famine in terms of time, money and energy. While their partners often love their happy-go-lucky disposition, they can be frustrated with the playmates' lack of long-term planning.

Easy going by nature, playmates are very accepting of their mates. They themselves enjoy freedom to do as they please. They don't want to be confined or changed, and are usually able to adjust to their partners' flaws. Playmates are the most tolerant to nagging of all the temperaments and they will initially change to please their partner, but the change is usually temporary. They are who they are. Constant nagging will eventually wear playmates down and they will seek escape before they will yield.

While some playmates are quieter, many like to be centre stage. They can be incredibly entertaining and are gifted storytellers. They bring laughter to any relationship. Their love of show can also lead them to extravagant acts of courtship, even once the relationship is committed. Even more low key playmates like to make an impact, through humour or by impressing a partner with their abilities.   However, this emphasis on impact can also be a playmate's strongest weapon in a disagreement, as they can cut their mate to bits in an instant.

Playmates are down-to-earth people. They talk in the here and now about concrete things, and their language tends to be coloured with colloquialisms. They love possibilities, but usually based on what you can see, hear and touch. Their concreteness stems from their acute awareness of sensory information. They take in all the sights, sounds, and smells in an environment and notice things like subtle nuances of body language. A playmate's sensory hunger, as well as their warm and fun-loving personality, can cause their eyes to stray. Their mates may become upset at their inclination to flirt, and in fairness, it is difficult for them to deny their impulses.

Playmates' edgy style and comfort with the physical world often draw them to physical activities or gaming challenges. They love adventure and risk. The stakes are rarely daunting to a playmate. They also find stimulation in toys and gadgets. They have amazing tactile abilities and enjoy working with their hands.

Playmates suffer stress when they feel confined or stuck in a state of boredom. Their drive to make an impact intensifies and even a negative impact will do. Playmates may also yield to their sensory cravings and indulge themselves in some way. In order to get out of their mood, playmates need to be allowed freedom for their creativity.

Helpmates

When the satisfaction or the security of another person becomes as significant to one as one's own satisfaction or security, then the state of love exists.

Henry Stack Sullivan

Helpmates are the true guardians of the home and hearth. While they will go along with the social norms of the dating game and have a good time, they tend to want to settle down. They look forward to the comforts of a mate and a family. In fact, helpmates run the risk of taking the dating game a bit too seriously and may immediately judge each date by the standards of a mate. While helpmates are normally cautious about making commitments, they may also run the risk of feeling they should domesticate. As a result, they may enter into a relationship for the purpose of organizing a household.

Helpmates are extremely attractive mates because they do put their home and family first. A happy household is a very fulfilling achievement for them. Helpmates see themselves as providers and protectors of the home. Diligence and promptness are key to their work ethic. You cannot tell a helpmate to be irresponsible – they would be overridden with guilt if they did not fulfill their duties and obligations. They are loyal and dependable mates who follow through on their promises.

Helpmates have a knack for handling logistics and see to it that their households run smoothly and efficiently. They look after the details others often forget. However, they may scold a mate and remind them of what they 'should' have done. With a natural economic sense, helpmates also manage household resources with neither waste nor haste. However, they do like to accumulate material possessions and may fall into 'keeping up with the Jones'. Helpmates can also be methodical, as they like standardized, tried and true procedures. They trust experience and what they have done in the past. To maximize efficiency, helpmates will implement such structures and processes within a household to manage the details of daily life. However, they run the risk of over-structuring their lives. Combined with their habit of worrying over their responsibility, they may lose sight of having fun in a relationship.

It is not only the household aspect that is key to the helpmate, but the union of the people in the home. It is important for helpmates to feel they are part of a family environment. They do prefer some type of hierarchy to exist within the family structure, but they want unity in the group. Helpmates value their roots and want to pass their heritage on to their children. They are often ones who uphold traditions and look to the past with fondness. Passing on their family values and morals is also seen as a joy and responsibility. Helpmates have a definite sense of right and wrong, and that differs from the soulmate sense of ethics. Unlike soulmates, helpmates will abide by externally defined rules for the singular justification that they believe rules are put there for a reason. Helpmates are also always there to offer support to their loved ones and they enjoy being needed. They want to work with their mate to make decisions and would be upset if they were left out of the process.

Helpmates are grounded people and their conversation reflects this practicality. More conventional in their nature, they like to talk of practical subjects not abstract flights of fancy. They also tend to recount information from beginning to end in their normal structured manner. Their language is also more formal, though in social setting they fall into group norms.

Helpmates usually join clubs or groups affiliated with their interests, as camaraderie is important to them. Their sense of responsibility may also draw them to civic and religious groups. Helpmates also enjoy hands-on activities of the home like cooking, building or crafts.

Helpmates fall under stress when they are excluded from the group and when they are taken advantage of for their helpfulness. When excluded from the group they need to be brought in again or to find a new membership. If they feel they are being used or a partner is not upholding his/her responsibilities, helpmates may fall into complaining and nagging. They will project doom and gloom scenarios onto everything. In this case, the others need to show appreciation for the helpmate and demonstrate responsibility through action.

Mindmates

To live is like to love – all reason is against it, and all healthy instinct for it.

Samuel Butler

Mindmates are intellectually rigorous individuals who want to meet their mental match in a mate. Some are too engrossed in their work to play the dating game, others excitedly partake confident of their courting abilities. However, all approach serious relationships knowing that a mate must stimulate the intellect as much as the heart. Sometimes mindmates attract adoring listeners and will take on the role of 'instructor', but such relationships usually won't last, as the mindmate will find little challenge mentally. Cerebral interplay is a strong aphrodisiac for this temperament, and a mate must at least command respect as a capable individual.

The drive for knowledge and competence is central to mindmates and they are often frustrated when their expertise does not carry over into the relationship arena. They are frequently misunderstood as cold and dispassionate partners. On the contrary, however, they often feel deep affection for their loved ones, but are not as effusive about their regard as most mates would prefer.

Mindmates live in a world of theories and models, delighting in abstract ideas and thoughts. They are irreverent free thinkers talented at design and implementation. In fact, mindmates are often engrossed in their contemplation to the point that they are unaware of the daily reality of people and objects. Not only do they forget the little things like saying, 'I love you', or picking up the dry-cleaning, but they may even forget anniversaries. In addition to this absentmindedness, mindmates hate redundancy. Once they have firmly committed to a relationship, they see no need to constantly reaffirm the obvious with imprecise and ill-defined words such as 'I love you'. Caring and support are demonstrated by helping mates to analyze and solve their problems and through respect for their competence. Mindmates will often move to work out a logical solution or attempt to disprove their mates,' negative feelings, rather than listen and comfort their partner. To the mindmate it is not efficient to 'wallow' in the problem. Instead, their focus on effectiveness drives them to take action towards a resolution.

When dealing with issues of their own, mindmates rarely reach out for help. They have a strong sense of autonomy and prefer to create their own destiny. Asking for help would make them feel incompetent. This autonomy also allows the mate a large degree of freedom. Mindmates don't expect or want dependency in their relationship, but instead believe strongly in being their own person. They are hardly ever possessive or jealous.

Seeing the world through logical eyes, mindmates strive to understand, predict and explain. They may become quite effective at inferring the interworkings of their partner's mind, but more often they are perplexed by the unpredictability of human behaviour. Emotional outbursts and illogical reasoning do not compute in their minds. Mindmates pride themselves on self-control and expect it in others. They prefer to discuss issues calmly and rationally. They are also strong critical thinkers. They believe it is helpful to point out flaws in logic and reasoning, which sometimes upsets their mates who see this as criticism.

Mindmates also enjoy debate and may goad a partner into a contest of wit for amusement. In general, they tend to gravitate towards cerebral interests such as reading, puzzles, strategy games, or quiz shows. Whatever the interest, they will strive to master it. Mindmates also have an affinity to the latest and greatest tools and technologies. They admire innovation and efficiency of design.

When stressed, mindmates begin to question their own competence. They feel incapable and stupid. As a result, they may lose their motivation or plunge even harder into their work only to get tangled up in the details. The needed antidote is reassurance of their abilities and a new project where their expertise is valued.

Soulmates

Love demands the impossible, the absolute, the sky on fire, inexhaustible springtime, life after death, and death itself transfigured into eternal life.

Albert Camus

Soulmate describes this temperament because they are the most idealistic of all in looking for a mate. They are unwavering in their crusade for 'the one' and want more than just a companion, friend or lover. They want and need a spiritual union with their partner – a special closeness and soulful bonding. Constantly questing for their own purpose and identity, soulmates see discovering a mate as finding a part that will help complete them.

In this search, they can have a tendency to project their ideal image of a mate onto a special person, only to be desperately disappointed when the mirage fades. Sometimes the relationship cannot survive this disillusionment and the soulmate may temporarily swear off finding a mate altogether, or move on to repeat the process in a string of serial monogamy. If the relationship does survive, the soulmate may view it as a cherished project, aimed towards the fruition of the ideal.

As relationships are central to them, soulmates can be deeply caring companions. Future-oriented, they focus on the development of the relationship and those involved in it. However, this future focus can sometimes prevent them from enjoying the present or savouring the past. Instead, they live in the world of hope. Valuing uniqueness, they see the strengths and latent abilities of their loved ones and strive to help them achieve their potential. Their faith and belief in those they love rarely wavers.

Soulmates are also acutely self-aware, not necessarily of their bodies like playmates, but of the 'self'. They enjoy inner exploration. Just as they endeavour to develop others, they strive towards self-actualization. Aside from intimate romantic outings, soulmates will often want their partners to accompany them to classes, workshops, or lessons around their interests and passions. They may also encourage volunteering and champion social and environmental issues. Soulmates have strong self-defined ethics and values, and wrestle over dilemmas of conscience more than any other temperament. Realism often crashes into their idealism.

Soulmates are also strong and diplomatic communicators who enjoy exploring feelings, personal beliefs, dreams, fantasies and ideas. In relationships, soulmates expect deep and intimate communication. A robotic 'yes, dear . . .' is likely to get a mate into a lot of trouble, as soulmates are keenly aware of inauthenticity. They can't stand fake and superficial conversation. Soulmates are also empathic communicators. They are aware of even the slightest nuance of emotion and feel the pain of their partners. This sensitivity makes conflict agonizing for them and, in general, soulmates tend to avoid tense situations. However, when their values are crossed as they can be in a relationship, they may lash out with uncontrollable fury or go right for the emotional throat of their partner. Their emotional acuity can also cause soulmates to become overwhelmed by emotional concerns, and as a result they may deal ineffectively with their partner's support needs at times. If their mate becomes too needy they may even become frustrated and push them away to 'stand on their own'. Soulmates may need constant support and reaffirmation to deal with their emotional crises, as well as their constant questioning of the self.

When stressed soulmates can appear hypersensitive, clingy, and paranoid believing that the world and even their mates are against them. They may also disconnect when a relationship grows tense. The needed antidote is nurturing and support from the partner. A new cause or quest to fulfill their need for meaning can also re-energize them.

You can't escape who you are

Our temperament is like a lens that filters and colours the way we see the world. To walk in someone else's shoes is nearly impossible, as you must change the way you perceive the world. However, as we progress through this book with our knowledge of temperament we will aim to make the material interesting and useful to each lovemate by including:

◆ Concrete exercises and examples for playmates and helpmates.
◆ Theory and a framework for mindmates.
◆ A people focus for soulmates.

As you read this book, become aware of the sections that you gravitate to more – could be a good indicator of your temperament!

Case Studies

In the following two case studies, we follow two couples as they initially assess their temperament and loving style, and then as they move on to profiling the relationship. The purpose of these case studies is to show how this profiling approach works in real life.

Joan and Bill

Joan and Bill had been dating seriously for five years, living together in a committed, long-term relationship. They attended a couples workshop because they were interested in learning more about each other against the backdrop of style and temperament. Both of them had a very limited knowledge of type and temperament before the session.

When Joan was introduced to the lovemates, she initially gravitated towards helpmate and soulmate, because both were people-focused, however she had 'tested' as a mindmate.

Bill believed strongly, based on the descriptions and the tables, that he was a mindmate, because he gravitated to the objective analysis described there. However he also felt some connection with the playmate, because of the requirement for freedom and the need to produce concrete, tangible results. He thought that mindmates sounded a little more academic in approach than he was.

Many people find evidence of themselves in more than one lovemate: a natural phenomenon. The challenge rests in trying to identify what is really important to you, and what is adapted behaviour. When they each reviewed the other's selection, Bill saw Joan's idealism, the desire to do the right thing, the ethics and the nurturing of potential as strong indicators for soulmate. In addition, when Joan read the description, her dislike of inauthenticity such as 'the robotic yes' from her mate, struck a chord and indicated that the behaviour he observed from Joan was more consistent with soulmate. This feedback loop proved really valuable in helping Joan to sort accurately.

In terms of Bill being able to narrow down his choice to either mindmate or playmate, he indicated that his response tended to vary with the situation (a very playmate thing to say as they are contextual thinkers: their approach varies depending on the situation in which they find themselves). He wanted more concrete data before making a selection. Although Bill was unable to decide between the two lovemates, Joan's input was valuable in helping him observe his own actions.

So as they moved onto reviewing their loving style, Joan decided to explore soulmate further and Bill to evaluate mindmate and playmate in more depth. We will continue this case study in the next chapter. Over one third of couples do not sort accurately when they first review temperament: the quandrants can appear too broad for selection, and many of these needs and abilities tend to reside in unconscious competence or incompetence. Self-knowledge is a complex subject. Input from our partner can help immensely in the discovery process!

'I have had more trouble with myself than with any other man I have met.'

On the Difficulty of Self-Assessment, Dwight L. Moody

Logan and Patricia

Logan and Patricia had been together for five years and married for two. Both had been married before, and Patricia had a daughter from her first marriage. Together they had one son and they were expecting another child. They attended a couples workshop because Logan had been introduced to temperament and type at work, and he thought this knowledge would be useful in making their relationship more productive. Both were deeply committed to the other, but were experiencing some conflicts managing the other work and family pressures in their life.

Logan had quickly gravitated towards the mindmate temperament in the initial session he attended for the following reasons:

◆ People who worked with him valued his objective analysis: he was usually able to produce a logical argument for a course of action.

◆ He would create a clearly articulated strategy and action plan for his team although his team often said that he was not always aware of the detailed implementation steps that were required to make the strategy a reality.

◆ He constantly questioned approaches and systems to improve them. This critical thinking ability is always a good indicator for mindmate.

One of the benefits that Logan and his team experienced from profiling the personalities was to gain a clearer understanding of the mindmate's strengths and how to work more positively with this knowledge. He hoped that this would translate into his interactions with Patricia.

Patricia, on the other hand, gravitated towards helpmate and soulmate because of the people interest demonstrated by both lovemates. She felt the helpmate was a little too 'rule bound' for her, but at the same time she felt the soulmate was a little too abstract and intangible. She also saw some of the playmate in her liking of fun and socialising. When she read Logan's description, it crystallised for her many of the factors that she enjoyed about him, and many that she tended to take personally in their interaction. Logan was unsure whether he thought that her driving forces were more like helpmate or soulmate.

As a result, Logan entered the next step convinced he was a mindmate, and Patricia with the intention of sorting accurately between helpmate and soulmate. We will pick up their self-assessment process in the next chapter. _____

Discussion points

1. Based on the self-assessment that you have completed, what do you perceive to be your temperament?
2. When you consider your partner or previous people with

whom you have had relationships, what do you perceive to be their temperaments?

Summary

In this chapter we have introduced the concepts of temperament to not only help us understand what we look for in a relationship, but also what we are attracted to and value in a partner. You learned the following about personality differences:

- There are four lovemates or temperaments, which have been described for over 25 centuries. These lovemates can provide us with a simple insight into what is important to us, and what may frustrate us in a relationship.
- These lovemates are:
  - The playmate who constantly seeks immediate concrete action to take in a restriction-free world.
  - The helpmate who looks after the family and provides stability and consistency.
  - The mindmate who constantly seeks the logical operating principles to control their own destiny.
  - The soulmate who constantly searches for meaningful interactions and purpose in life.
- By understanding and valuing these differences we can capitalise on our relationship strengths, versus focusing on our weaknesses to build a viable long-term partnership.

However, as we observed in the case studies, four lovemates are not enough to define all the differing aspects of human behaviour. In the next chapter we will describe how we may differ from our partner in the ways we gather information and make decisions.

CHAPTER 2

Loving in Your Own Style

I n Chapter 1 we discovered what kind of lovemate you are, and possibly what kind of lovemate you have! This awareness of our temperament was the first step in understanding ourselves and improving our relationships. However, while temperament theory is very enlightening, it cannot explain the full depth of personality alone. We need to look through another lens to develop a more focused picture of ourselves and the way we approach relationships.

In this chapter we will learn about our **functions** and our **loving style**, which provide insight into how we gather information, make decisions and orient ourselves in the world. We will also revisit the case studies from Chapter 1 to demonstrate how each couple views data and makes decisions differently based on the chemistry of their loving styles.

From lovemates to loving styles

While an underlying pattern of each lovemate clearly exists, there is still a wide range of varying behaviour within any of these four temperaments. For example, two playmates may recognise their similar motivation, but see things very differently when making a key family decision. While there are many factors that influence who we are such as education, family background, or culture, there is also another innate element to personality: our **type**. Type theory looks at our cognitive functions around gathering information and making decisions, as well as our orientation to the internal or external world.

There are eight cognitive functions, which we all use with varying ease. It is the natural adroitness with which we use these functions that creates different personality types. These differing personality types are what we call loving styles in relationships. Where temperament influences what is important to us, loving styles show how we approach our relationship.

> 'We know what a person thinks not when he tells us what he thinks but by his actions.'
>
> *Isaac Bashevis Singer*

Understanding functions

The Swiss psychologist Carl Jung developed the concept of cognitive functions. Jung recognised four differing ways of gathering information and four differing ways of making decisions, producing eight functions. Jung saw that different individuals preferred one function to the other when gathering information or making decisions, ie. the function was more natural or more consistently used. The eight approaches we use to gather information and make decisions are listed below. We will review them in more detail later.

Information gathering			
Sensing		**Intuiting**	
Experiencing	Recalling	Brainstorming	Visioning
Decision-making			
Thinking		**Feeling**	
Systematizing	Analyzing	Harmonizing	Valuing

Try it now: **Using your left and right hand**

Write your name using your 'preferred' hand (the one you normally write with – right or left).

Now write your name using your 'weaker' hand (the one you rarely write with).

What differences did you notice? How did it feel? What was difficult/easy? You probably found writing with your preferred hand:

- much easier
- quicker
- required less concentration and energy
- appeared with smoothness and clarity.

On the other hand, you probably found writing with your less preferred hand:

- more difficult
- slower, jerky and/or awkward
- required more energy and concentration
- felt undeveloped – as if you were back in school.

The exercise above serves as an awareness builder for the differences in accessing our preferred functions over our non-preferred functions. Much like signing your name with your usual hand, your preferred functions require less energy to use, demand less conscious thought, and are more comfortable, while writing with your other hand feels more awkward, just like your non-preferred functions.

In addition, *while we each have all eight functions, some functions are easier for us to access and use than others.* A preference for a function, just like handedness, is an unconscious mental orientation or habit of the mind manifesting in individual differences. It is not the same as a conscious choice or liking one thing more than another.

Everyone uses all these mental tools to some degree in daily life. Rather like a ball in a pinball machine, we bounce from using one function to another in rapid succession. However, just as some of the pinball bumpers are larger so we hit them more often, there are functions that are more present for us to use, and as a result we tend to unconsciously favour them.

Functions in action: organizing a wedding

Before we define and explore each function in depth, consider the following example. If you were in charge of organizing a wedding, the process might push you to use all eight functions. Examples of how these functions might be used are listed in the diagram on page 23.

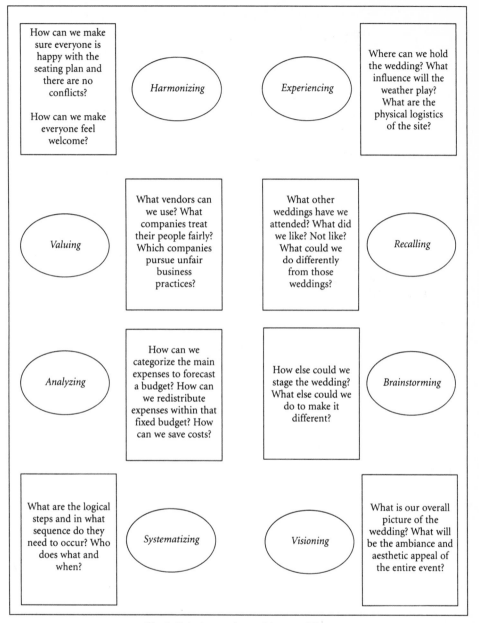

Fig. 2. Functions and organizing a wedding.

Discovering your functions

In the next sections of this chapter we introduce you to each of
these information-gathering and decision-making functions to
enable you to assess which functions appear the most comfortable
for you to use. Understanding the functions you use easily will

provide you with greater insight into your own strengths and weaknesses. In turn, comparing and contrasting the functions you and your partner use will lead to a clearer comprehension of possible connection and conflicts between you.

Lovemates and their functions

The way individuals access different functions creates the variation within a group of the same temperament. People who share the same temperament may access different information gathering functions and use differing decision-making functions, which creates eight loving styles. The table below shows how the four lovemates become eight based on the functions they use. (Orientation will later show us how we reach 16!)

Temperament/ lovemate	Function for gathering data	Function for making decisions		Loving style
Playmate	Experiencing	Analyzing	or*	Manoeuvring Playmate
		Valuing		Improvizing Playmate
Helpmate	Recalling	Systematizing	or	Regulating Helpmate
		Harmonizing		Nurturing Helpmate
Mindmate	Brainstorming	Analyzing		Innovating Mindmate
	Visioning	or	Systematizing	Marshalling Mindmate
Soulmate	Brainstorming	Valuing		Advocating Soulmate
	Visioning	or	Harmonizing	Actualizing Soulmate

*Once the 'or' decision is made the path proceeds horizontally across the row to the loving style.

Information-gathering functions

Learning about sensing and intuiting

The information-gathering functions describe how each person gathers or perceives information. If we prefer a **sensing** function, we tend to primarily gather information through our senses using sight, sound, smell, touch, taste and balance. We tend to trust whatever can be measured or documented and what is real and concrete. If we prefer an **intuiting** function we gather information through ideas, patterns, possibilities, hypotheses and inferred meanings. We tend to trust abstract concepts, ideas, and hunches, minimizing the importance of practical data. Playmates and helpmates tend to use more sensory data, and mindmates and soulmates tend to use more intuitive data.

> 'I never notice whas has been done. I only see what remains to be done.'
>
> *Marie Curie* (describes the difference between concrete and abstract)

Assessing sensing and intuiting

Look through the list below and see which appears to be the better fit for you. You don't need to associate with each characteristic but you will probably gravitate to one column.

Sensing	Intuiting
◆ Tune into information that is concrete and real: see hear, smell, touch, taste and feel	◆ Tune into information that is abstract or theoretical: concepts, theories, patterns and insights
◆ Notice concrete details like changes in a mate's appearance; can be frustrated when mate is oblivious to the concrete environment	◆ Notice and interpret what's between the lines in communication; can be frustrated when mate takes things literally
◆ Like to use tangible, physical or practical skills	◆ Like to philosophise and develop new concepts
◆ Tend to be specific: give details and examples in a linear step-by-step approach or in literal form	◆ Tend to be figurative with general descriptions and theories, using analogies and metaphors
◆ Speak and hear literally	◆ Speak and hear figuratively
◆ Tend to present concrete evidence either sequentially or briefly and to the point	◆ Tend to present information in impressions or organised around a conceptual framework without concrete examples
◆ Move from specific to general: start with the steps and move to the end result	◆ Move from general to specific: start with the end result and then build up the steps
◆ Can appear realistic or too focused on the details	◆ Can appear visionary or impractical
◆ Intimacy is in the details	◆ Intimacy is intuitive
◆ Love can be demonstrated through action	◆ Love is a concept difficult to describe

Delving deeper into information-gathering

Now that we have looked at sensing and intuiting, let's look at the two versions of each:

◆ The two versions of gathering data using sensing are **experiencing**, used strongly by playmates, and **recalling**, used strongly by helpmates. (See the table on page 24.)

◆ The two versions of gathering data using intuiting are **brainstorming**, used strongly by certain mindmates and soulmates, and **visioning**, again used strongly by other mindmates and soulmates.

The table below provides descriptions of each of these information-gathering functions.

INFORMATION-GATHERING PROCESSES			
Sensing		Intuiting	
Experiencing	Recalling	Brainstorming	Visioning
◆ Moving outward for the acute uptake of sensory data (sight, sound, touch, taste, smell and balance) and seeing new options in the now moment.	◆ Moving inward to recall past experiences and compare the present information to a rich historical data bank.	◆ Moving to the outer world for the unlimited exploration of new ideas and the perceptions of patterns and meanings.	◆ Moving inward for the unconscious correlation of conceptual ideas, possibilities and symbols that enter consciousness as a whole system or idea.
Playmate	*Helpmate*	*Mindmate/ Soulmate*	*Mindmate/ Soulmate*

Try it now

Assessing information-gathering-functions

Work out the extent to which you use each function by giving yourself a score for each question:

always = 5

sometimes = 3

seldom = 1

never = 0

The results should help you assess which information-gathering function is the most comfortable for you. If it is difficult to self-evaluate, it may help to have your partner or a friend provide input.

Function: Experiencing

1. Are you **acutely** tuned in to the external universe (sound, sight, smell, taste, touch, movement, etc)?
2. Do you pride yourself on your physical acuity, rarely if ever having a physical accident or clumsiness?
3. Do you see options in the moment?
4. Can you read minute changes in body language?
5. Do you have an innate aesthetic sense?
6. Do you quickly know what the other person wants and how you could provide it for them?

Function: Recalling

1. When starting a new project do you immediately think back to a similar situation you experienced before?
2. Does your memory play like videotape, as you clearly remember details and occurrences?
3. Do you recall and describe past events in linear sequence?
4. Do you naturally compare and contrast the current data to the past to determine such things as better or worse, higher or lower?
5. When assessing risks, to what extent do you put in safeguards knowing something will go wrong?
6. In relationships, do you create ground rules and peramaters for you and your partner?

Function: Brainstorming

1. Do you naturally think of numerous possibilities when starting a project?
2. Do you have a desire to bounce your ideas off someone?
3. When you start with an idea do you verbally brainstorm 'what if' 'what else' scenarios?
4. When discussing plans and strategies do you consider unusual possibilities or methods to accomplish them?
5. Do you easily read between the lines and see hidden patterns and meanings?

6. Do your ideas come to you in bits and pieces that you keep building on?

Function: Visioning

1. If you are asked to come up with ideas in the moment, do you need to take a mental step back to reflect and allow the idea to gel?
2. How often do you wrestle with a problem only to have a complete solution come to you in the middle of the night or when you are not consciously working on the problem?
3. When you come up with an idea, does it come as a flash of inspiration?
4. Do you trust your picture to the extent that you take certain risks that others would not?
5. Do you always see the end result as a complete picture or solution and then work to put the necessary support in place?
6. Are you sometimes frustrated by your inability to articulate the steps you took in coming up with a solution?

Total your scores for each information-gathering function. Your highest total should give you some indication of your main information-gathering function, but use your best judgment in this decision.

Functions in action

Let's look at how these functions could appear in relationships.

'I notice everything in the environment – appearance, smells, textures, noises, tastes. There are things I just know; I'm not even conscious that I have noticed it. This can make me an attentive, nurturing partner – I can anticipate needs and be there with the right fix, even before my partner knows there is a need. It can also make me an obnoxious know-it-all. I love excitement, stimulation and to experience things fully – adventures, good food and wine, parties, touching, art, music and conversation. This can be a point of frustration when my partner does not want to participate and I can annoy my partner by focusing on my environment, rather than them.'

On **Experiencing** in relationships

'Whenever we are making decisons looking at the future, I like to look back to where we have come from, and other similar experiences we have had as a couple. For instance, when we were deciding to move house, I wanted to change for the better. I tend to remember significant events almost minute by minute; these are normally centred on holidays, Christmas, things we have done together and events with family.'

On **Recalling** in relationships

'I get excited about the future with my partner and am always thinking about the ways we could be together. In our relationship we are both full of ideas, but I tend to gravitate towards what we haven't done before. I think just about anything is possible and I can talk about an idea's endless possibilities. We are also great sounding boards for each other. When either of us has an idea we discuss it and it just snowballs. Sometimes our eagerness to say what we have to say can lead us to talk over each other.'

On **Brainstorming** in relationships

'I have a very vivid picture in my head about what people in love do, say and how they behave towards each other. Unfortunately, this can be a source of disappointment when my partner does not share my vision. In addition I always have a picture about what the future will look like: where we would live, what work I would do, what books I should write, and then I am internally driven to make these a reality. I know this is sometimes frustrating for my partner, because it is hard to attach concrete data to the idea, and he often struggles to understand why this was the only way to approach the situation as far as I am concerned. Luckily my partner has learned to expect and deal with that!'

On **Visioning** in relationships

Decision-making approaches

Learning about thinking and feeling

The second set of Jung's cognitive functions relates to how we make decisions and come to conclusions. Decisions based on

thinking tend to be made impersonally, logically and analytically. We see criteria as black and white: 'the facts, just the facts!' If we make decisions based on **feeling**, we are more interested in subjective criteria such as personal values, the people involved, and special circumstances. We see criteria as shades of grey. Both are rational decision-making processes, they are simply based on different criteria.

Assessing thinking and feeling

All mindmates tend to use thinking data primarily, while all soulmates tend to use mostly feeling data. Playmates and helpmates vary. Look through the list below and see which appears to be the better fit for you. You don't need to associate with each characteristic but will probably gravitate to one column.

Thinking	Feeling
◆ Feelings need to be understood to be truly felt	◆ Feelings are felt and often difficult to explain
◆ Evaluate mate and self for ways to improve	◆ Support mate and self and avoid discussing faults
◆ Conflict can be intriguing	Conflict is gut-wrenching
◆ Need to be in control of their emotions	◆ Like to be swept away in emotion, need to express their emotions
◆ Intimacy is to be dissected, analyzed and improved upon	◆ Intimacy is to be appreciated for what it is: a form of selflessness
◆ Logical analysis	◆ Emotional intensity
◆ Remember numbers and figures more easily	◆ Remember faces and names more easily
◆ Decisions are based on logical, objective criteria	◆ Decisions are based on personal, subjective criteria
◆ Definition of fairness is one standard for all	◆ Definition of fairness is caring and based on personal factors
◆ Others say I sometimes appear heartless, insensitive and uncaring	◆ Others say I sometimes appear over-emotional, illogical and weak

'Your reason and your passion are the rudder and sails of your seafaring soul. If either your sails or your rudder be broken, you can but toss and drift, or else be held at a standstill in mid-seas. For reason alone, is a force confining; and passion unattended, is a flame that burns to its own destruction.'

On thinking and feeling, *The Prophet,* Kahlil Gibran

Delving deeper into the decision-making functions

Now that we have looked at thinking and feeling, let's look at the two versions of each:

♦ The two versions of making decisions using thinking are **systematizing,** used strongly by certain helpmates and mindmates and **analyzing,** used strongly by certain playmates and mindmates. (See the table on page 24)

♦ The two versions of making decisions using feeling are **harmonizing,** (used strongly by certain helpmates and soulmates) and **valuing,** strongly used by certain playmates and soulmates.

Descriptions for each of the decision-making functions are in the table below.

DECISION-MAKING PROCESSES			
Thinking		Feeling	
Systematizing	Analyzing	Harmonizing	Valuing
♦ Making decisions using logical objective criteria to organize, structure and achieve goals in the external world.	♦ Making decisions where information gathered is evaluated and sorted against an internal mental model.	♦ Making decisions using subjective criteria to optimize interpersonal harmony in the external world.	♦ Making decisions based on personal subjective values and an internal belief system.

Try it now:

Assessing decision-making functions

Work out the extent to which you use each function by giving yourself a score for each question:

always = 5
sometimes = 3
seldom = 1
never = 0

The results should help you begin to assess which decision-making function is the most comfortable for you. If it is difficult to self-evaluate, it may help to have your partner or a friend provide input.

Function: Systematizing

1. Do you like to structure and organise the external world based on a predetermined end result?
2. Are you skilled in taking a project through a systematic, step-by-step replicable process?
3. Do you place clear boundaries in the external world, eg I will do this, but not that?
4. Do you rely on published facts and data in the external world to make decisions?
5. Do you organize things by categories, colours, sizes, types, etc?
6. Do you make lists of pros and cons and then push for a decision?

Function: Analyzing

1. Do you internally consider facts and data to develop your own rationale?
2. Do you sometimes find your logic is at odds with others'?
3. Do you innately categorize data internally?
4. When you have an opinion do you stick to it, arguing based on logical deductions?
5. Do you pull inwards to analyse different options and approaches?
6. Once you have made an important decision, is it really hard for you to change that decision?

Function: Harmonizing

1. In individual and group interactions, are you aware of everyone's feelings?
2. Do you prefer that everyone be in agreement with a decision or that the decision be made in the best interest of the group?
3. Do you find conflict extremely stressful and try to avoid it and restore harmony where possible?
4. Do you tend to self-disclose and talk to others about personal situations?
5. Can you appear gushy and warm?
6. Do people say that you show all your emotions on your face?

Function: Valuing

1. Do you act in accordance with strongly held internal opinions and beliefs?
2. Are you hesitant or embarrassed to explain those beliefs to others?
3. When your belief system is challenged do you react strongly or make drastic decisions, eg leave a job because your ethics are offended?
4. Do you strive to live by your values and struggle when values conflict? Do you strive to interject those values into your mate?
5. Have you been accused of making decisions devoid of logic when you know you are doing the right thing?
6. Do you run situations through a 'how would that make me feel' criteria when reacting?

Total your score for each decision-making function. Your highest total should give you some indication of your main decision-making function, but use your best judgement in this decision. Again, get feedback from your partner to help you.

Functions in action

Let's look at how these functions could appear in relationships.

'When we are approaching major life decisions, my immediate reaction is to map out the options, each with its own set of pros and cons, and list them all – with contributing factors – on a matrix. Before we make any value judgements I want to see the big picture in an organized fashion. This can be frustrating for my partner who likes to act on gut feel, therefore over time I have learnt to conduct this process much more in my head. I also like to structure my weekends – there's always so much to get done. I create and manage a "to do" list, although I have been trying to make sure I add fun to that list.'

On **Systematizing** in relationships

'I am constantly assessing the verbal information my partner relays to me. At times, it appears I haven't heard anything that has been said. During the silence I have sorted the data into several categories or approaches, on which I then provide my viewpoint. Sometimes this feedback is seen as overly critical when it was supposed to be a relaxing conversation. With any data, I check for the underlying principle and check it for consistency. If I perceive the data is inconsistent, I will question to verify the logic.'

On **Analyzing** in relationships

'In our relationship, I try to ensure that my partner and I are in agreement and I normally am fairly tuned into his feelings if he is upset. If we are both stressed, it can be difficult because we both feel the other's pain and we don't have an objective perspective sometimes. I have a sense of what I think is the sensitive or right thing to say for a relationship, and if this standard is not met, I can certainly show my feelings. I am able to self-disclose examples from my experience to form a connection with my mate when I am empathising.'

On **Harmonizing** in relationships

'There are certain things I believe in and when my partner offends me in one of these beliefs we have a problem. I usually measure most things by this belief system: "how would I feel in this situation?" I also try to influence my partner by discussing my beliefs around the issues that we are facing and I appreciate the conversation because it helps me to clarify something that I feel. In addition, I struggle with my values in terms of how I will live up to them completely. My partner and I have numerous discussions about the pressure I put on myself.'

On **Valuing** in relationships

Direction of energy

Defining extroversion and introversion

A critical set of differences, apart from functions, that was outlined by Jung is the orientation for **introverting** or **extroverting**. When we add this final dimension, our eight loving styles grow to 16, as we have an extroverted and introverted version of each.

Unfortunately, extroverting and introverting carry the baggage of a stereotypical set of behaviours. For instance, we often consider those with an extroverting preference to be gregarious, talkative, loud and sociable, and introverting with those who are quiet, shy, unsociable and reclusive. In reality you will find many gregarious introverts and many shy extroverts! It is important to step away from these connotations in order to truly understand the meaning of introverting and extroverting in the sense we will be using them in relationships and throughout this book.

Your flow of energy: extroverting/introverting preference

Many analysts of personality think of extroverting and introverting in terms of where you *get* your energy: from the outer world (extroverting) or the inner world (introverting). The common analogy is how you charge your batteries. This definition does not take temperament into account at all. An introverting soulmate may feel most energized when building a special relationship or getting involved in an organization that works to improve social conditions. In the same way, playmates naturally seek sensory data and therefore may still look extroverted even though they have an introverting preference. An individual is most content and energized when his/her core needs are being met.

It is more valuable to think of extroverting and introverting in terms of *what direction your energy naturally flows: externally or internally*, rather than its source.

In people with an extroverting preference energy naturally flows outwards to the external world of people and events. More time is spent initiating and externally processing.

In people with an introverting preference energy naturally flows inwards to ideas and thoughts. More time is spend in the inner world, receiving and reflecting.

To comprehend more fully the differences between extroverting and introverting, review the characteristic behaviours associated with each in the chart below. Then decide which orientation seems most like you.

Extroverting	Introverting
Often drawn out to interact	Often pulled in to reflect
Comfortable initiating relationships	Comfortable responding in relationships
Process information in the external world – talk out thoughts	Process information in the internal world – think out thoughts
Are easier to 'read': self-disclose readily	Are harder to 'read': share personal information with a few, close people
Talk more than listen	Listen more than talk
Communicate with enthusiasm	May keep enthusiasm to self
Use more expressive body language	Use more reserved body language
Many diverse relationships	Smaller number of in-depth relationships
Need outer world validation	Trust self-validation and insights

Tying it all together

The combination of our information-gathering and decision-making functions, and our introverting/extroverting orientations, create behaviour patterns or loving styles. With the addition of direction of energy, we now have a full picture of how the four lovemates become 16 loving styles. You probably use all of the information-gathering and decision-making functions at some time, but the two aligned with your temperament and loving style are more natural to you and easiest to use.

Temperament/ lovemate	Function for gathering data	Function for making decisions	Loving style	Loving style and orientation
Playmate Wants to see an immediate concrete tangible results and live in the present	*Experiencing* Gathering all the concrete data in the now moment	*Analyzing* Evaluating and sorting data against an internal model or	*Manoeuvring playmate* Manoeuvres to craft deals or solutions	*Extroverted Manoeuvrer* or* *Introverted Manoeuvrer*
		Valuing Making decisions against an internal values system	*Improvising playmate* Improvises to pull together talents and skills in the moment	*Extroverted Improvizer* or *Introverted Improvizer*
Helpmate Wants to have a clear role in the relationship and be respected for fulfilling their responsibility	*Recalling* Comparing and contrasting historical data to current data	*Systematizing* Making decisions based on logical criteria to plan in the external world	*Regulating helpmate* Regulates people and processes to ensure stability	*Extroverted Regulator* or *Introverted Regulator*
		Harmonizing Making decisions based on subjective criteria to optimize interpersonal harmony	*Nurturing helpmate* Nurtures within or even beyond home and hearth	*Extroverted Nurturer* or *Introverted Nurturer*

Temperament/ lovemate	Gather data	Make decisions	Love mate	Orientation
Mindmate Wants to be viewed as competent and able to create their own destiny	*Brainstorming* Unrestrained exploration of future patterns and possibilities	*Analyzing* Evaluating and sorting data against an internal model	*Innovating Mindmate* Innovates ideas, theories and models to share or adapt	*Extroverted Innovator* — or* — *Introverted Innovator*
	— or —			
	Visioning Receiving future data as a complete picture or outcome	*Systematizing* Making decisions based on logical criteria tó plan in the external world	*Marshalling Mindmate* Strategically marshals people or ideas into order or place	*Extroverted Marshaller* — or — *Introverted Marshaller*
Soulmate Wants a purpose and a genuine connection with the important people in their life	*Brainstorming* Unrestrained exploration of future patterns and possibilities	*Valuing* Making decisions against an internal values system	*Advocating Soulmate* Advocates causes, beliefs and ideas expressively or gently	*Extroverted Advocate* — or — *Introverted Advocate*
	— or —			
	Visioning Receiving future data as a complete picture or outcome	*Harmonizing* Making decisions based on subjective criteria to optimize interpersonal harmony	*Actualizing Soulmates* Actualize potential in self and others through teaching, training and mentoring	*Extroverted Actualizer* — or — *Introverted Actualizer*

*Once the 'or' decision is made the path proceeds horizontally across the row to the loving style.

Try it now

Assessing your type

Chart your loving style by *moving horizontally* across the rows in the table above. While this process is detailed, research has shown that it is a more accurate form of assessment than just taking a written test.

> It was shocking to learn that we had our type wrong all this time, and then see ourselves in a totally different way. The combination of temperament and Jung archetypes really struck a chord with us.
>
> Feedback from a couple using this approach

Using the table on page 38:

1. Choose which temperament appeared to be the best fit from Chapter 1. If you are not sure, select two.
2. Look at the exercise you completed on information-gathering functions on pages 27–28. Choose the one that you appeared to use most frequently and be sure it aligns with the lovemate you have chosen.
3. Look at the exercise you completed on decision-making functions on pages 32–33. Choose the one that you appeared to use most frequently and be sure it aligns with the lovemate you have chosen.
4. Review whether you thought your flow of energy was naturally outwards (extroverting) or inwards (introverting). Find this choice in the corresponding row.
5. Read several loving style descriptions based on your selection of lovemate, functions and orientation.
6. Ask your partner what they think if you are still unsure of your loving style.
7. Read the Key Distinctions Table (page 40) to achieve greater clarity between commonly confused loving styles.

Loving styles descriptions

In the descriptions of loving styles in the appendix (page 191) are:

1. The name of the loving style.
2. The temperament and its core needs and values.
3. The function this style uses first to either gather information or make decisions: this is the strongest function we use, rather like writing with your preferred hand.
4. The function this style uses secondly to support the first function: the opposite type of function (eg information-gathering if the first function is decision-making and vice versa).
5. The functions that are third and fourth. They provide the shadow side to the first two functions. They may appear weaker, or distorted, when they are in this support position depending on the extent to which they have been developed in work and home life.
6. A description for each loving style written in paragraph format.

KEY DISTINCTIONS TABLE			
Confusion	Shared function/ similarity in approach	Questions to answer	Suggested solution
◆ Innovating Mindmate and ◆ Manoeuvring Playmate	*Analyzing* ◆ The need to evaluate and sort against an internal framework. ◆ Does this fit with my hypothesis?	◆ Do you look for concrete data and examples to compare with your internal analysis? ◆ Do you move quickly from analysis to action?	◆ If no: consider Innovating Mindmate ◆ If yes: consider Manoeuvring Playmate
◆ Improvizing Playmate and ◆ Advocating Soulmate	*Valuing* ◆ The need to take action in alignment with a strong internal values system. ◆ What are the values that I want to live my life by?	◆ Do you easily turn your beliefs into action rather than struggle with defining them?	◆ If yes: consider Improvizing Playmate ◆ If no: consider Advocating Soulmate
◆ Regulating Helpmate and ◆ Marshalling Mindmate	*Systematizing* ◆ Making decisions using logical data to organise and make plans in the external world. Who is going to do what by when?	◆ Do you tend to base your decisions around history, tradition, experience and concrete data?	◆ If yes: consider Regulating Helpmate ◆ If no: consider Marshalling Mindmate
◆ Nurturing Helpmate and ◆ Actualizing Soulmate	*Harmonizing* ◆ Making decisions in the external world to optimize interpersonal harmony. ◆ What's the best decision for the rest of the group?	◆ Are you motivated by your future vision of how to make the world a better place, and live up to your potential?	◆ If no: consider Nurturing Helpmate ◆ If yes: consider Actualizing Soulmate

Loving styles and relationships

In a relationship individuals often use different information-gathering and decision-making functions and, as a result, can appear to be acting at cross-purposes. In addition, their orientations can cause them to process and interact differently. Once we understand these cognitive processes, we can use this diversity as a strength to ensure all viewpoints are considered, rather than letting them become liabilities or a source of conflict. By understanding which partner is using which function, you will be able to recognise and overcome the conflicts that can appear to pull the relationship in different directions. These subjects will be discussed more in later chapters.

Case Studies_____

Joan and Bill continue the sorting process

After reviewing temperament, Joan was exploring the soulmate and Bill was exploring either mindmate or playmate.

When reviewing the functions Joan definitely gravitated towards the more abstract communication mode associated with intuiting. However, when reviewing the information-gathering functions, she scored high both on visioning and brainstorming and was unable to select which she thought was strongest for her. When reviewing the decision-making functions, she felt comfortable with the subjective-versus-objective criteria for decisions, but was split between harmonizing and valuing. On closer examination, she realised that she was confusing the soulmate's empathy for harmonizing, and that rather than group consensus, her internal values and beliefs system drove her decision-making process. Bill agreed, remarking 'I admire her ability to persevere under the most intense internal and external pressures while maintaining her integrity.' Her energy orientation was obviously internal: she needed time to internally process and her emotions did not show easily on her face. When she reviewed the description for introverting advocate, she found it reflected many characteristics about herself of which she had previously been aware but struggled to explain objectively.

When reviewing the functions Bill clearly selected experiencing, although he also felt in writing code, that he would get a 'flash of inspiration' the complete solution, that he then would use to create the necessary concrete data. (This process is very common for playmates as they use visioning as a shadow function to experiencing.) In reviewing the decision-making functions, he clearly selected analyzing: he said that much of his time would be spent in evaluating what he heard other people say, and using this data to update or develop his mental framework. As Joan clearly stated, 'Bill is usually the more logical person, whereas I am more non-linear and emotional.' Finally, like Joan, his direction of energy was definitely internal: in company he always carefully considered what he was going to say. Many of his more extroverted acquaintances also sometimes felt uncomfortable while he paused before answering. When Bill read the description of the introverting manoeuvrer, it helped him to comprehend the critical differences between himself and a mindmate, both in terms of concrete data as well as concise language and a drive to move from analysis to action.

Logan and Patricia continue the sorting process

After reviewing temperament, Logan had selected mindmate and Patricia was divided between helpmate and soulmate.

Logan immediately aligned with the visioning and systematizing functions of the marshaller, which can look somewhat like a playmate, with the push for closure, but the differentiating factors lie in the organised process of planning the future-focused, abstract data-gathering process. With his direction of energy being external, Logan settled as the extroverting marshaller.

With information-gathering functions, Patricia scored high on recalling, and with the decision-making functions she scored high on harmonizing. Her direction of energy was also external. When she reviewed the description of the nurturer she realised that the use of harmonizing had made her look 'less rule-bound' than the regulating helpmates, and had also made her gravitate towards soulmate. However, her concrete information-gathering, with her ability to review the historic perspective, made her feel comfortable with the extroverting nurturer.

> 'My husband immediately indentifies with playmate: he says the description is dead on. Best of all he feels like he finally 'fits' and that knowing his correct temperament and type gives him permission to be the way he is and know he's OK.'
>
> Comments about a playmate experiencing this process

In the next chapter, we examine the impact these differences could have on their relationships. As you can see, the identification of the functions that individuals use to gather information and make decisions helps to clarify temperament and loving style. Without this step many individuals tend to either sort incorrectly, or find the descriptions of their lovemate and loving style so far off that they sound more like a horoscope than reality! _____

Discussion points

1. How clear were you on the differing information-gathering functions? Which ones appeared effortless for you? Which did you struggle to understand? Which information-gathering function do you think your partner uses? How could this affect the communication in your relationship?
2. How clear were you on the different decision-making functions? Which ones seemed effortless for you? Which did you struggle to comprehend? How do you think using these differing functions could affect your relationship? What stress could it bring?
3. Which world are you naturally drawn to: the inner or outer? What impact might this have on your relationship?
4. To what extent do you feel clear on your style? Were you able to move horizontally across the table? Where did your partner finish up?
5. If you were unclear, to what extent were you able to clarify any confusions using the distinctions table on page 40.

Summary

- There are four information-gathering functions: experiencing and recalling (based on sensory data in the present or in the past), and brainstorming and visioning (based on intuitive patterns and pictures in the future).
- In addition, there are four decision-making approaches, systematizing and analyzing (using logical/thinking criteria), and harmonizing and valuing (using subjective/feeling criteria).
- All of us can use all eight functions, but we vary in the proficiency and ease with which we can access all eight. This variation creates eight personality types or loving styles, from the four lovemates.
- Normally we have preferences for one function primarily for gathering data, and one function primarily for making decisions.
- Further understanding whether you are naturally drawn to the external world (extroverting) or pulled in to the internal world (introverting) results in 16 different loving styles.

◆ Understanding this pattern of functions and the way we choose to interact with the environment is critical to understanding how we will act as part of a long-term partnership.

*By now I know
the things I
know. And do
the things I do,
And if you do
not like me so,
to hell, my love,
with you.
Dorothy Parker*

CHAPTER 3

Valuing Differences

In the first two chapters we concentrated mainly on building an understanding of ourselves. In this chapter we begin to examine the potential similarities and differences between you and your partner, in terms of personality, gender and life experience. We will see how some characteristics draw you to certain temperaments and how certain temperament traits can completely frustrate you. By recognizing and valuing the differences, we can learn to capitalise on the commonal aspect and reduce or work around the potential conflicts.

> 'After all these years I have grown to love and appreciate my partner. If she decides to make a change that is her call. We talk about her choice and when the talking is done she makes the change.'
>
> Appreciating the differences

Nature or nurture

Whenever we talk about differences between individuals, whether in a relationship or at work, the most commonly asked question is, 'Do I behave the way I do because that's my *nature* or because of things that have happened to me in my life – *nurture*?' The answer is *both*! Nurture and nature are two facets of being that are almost impossible to separate. If one study links behaviour to nature, another will find how nurture plays a role as well and vice versa. Even in the womb, the realm of nature, the mother's actions (nurturing) are affecting the infant.

Our personality also develops as a complex interaction of nurture and nature. While we believe that temperament and loving style are largely innate, character develops as our core personality interacts with the external environment, the nurture element in understanding differences.

'Nature never repeats herself, and the possibilities of one human soul will never be found in another.'

Elizabeth Cady Stanton

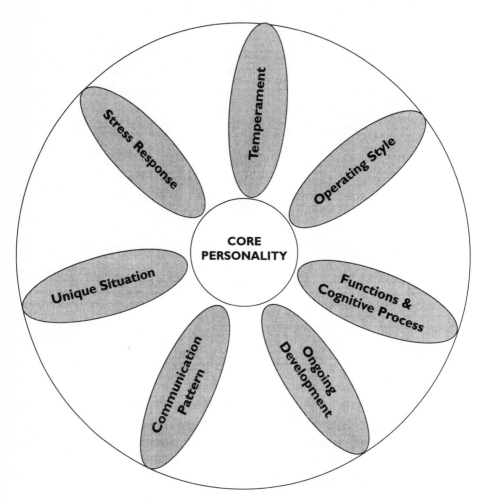

Fig. 3. TO FOCUS: the seven lenses of personality.

TO FOCUS: the seven lenses of personality

There are seven lenses in studying personality which help **TO FOCUS** and clarify the complex elements of human differences (see Figures 3 and 4):

♦ **T – temperament** reflecting our fundamental human needs and values. These are the four lovemates looked at in Chapter 1.

- ◆ O – **operating style,** or **loving style** as we call it in relationships. This lens clarifies how we prefer to operate and approach the world.
- ◆ F – **functions** originally described by Jung and organised in a hierarchy in our brain, affecting the way we perceive information and make decisions.
- ◆ O – **ongoing development** explains how each type develops over time.
- ◆ C – **communication pattern** refers to the different language used by each lovemate (we discuss this in Chapter 6).
- ◆ U – **unique situation** shows how each individual's culture, family, upbringing, education, location, etc can further explain personality differences.
- ◆ S – **stress response** covers how each lovemate and loving style responds to stress.

So far we have focused on temperament (the lovemates) and type (loving style). We will touch on other lenses throughout the book. Trying to examine one's own personality is like trying to focus a kaleidoscope; you can see many different pieces, but they are shifting constantly, each piece becoming clearer and then fading away. By taking a deeper look through these lenses we will gain a greater insight into our own and our partner's behaviour.

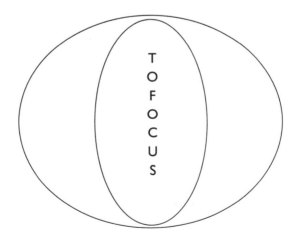

Fig. 4. TO FOCUS – focused.

'I could see depth, a hint and promise of more than was obvious. He seemed like a book worth reading and reading a second, third, fourth time. And every time I would see something a little differently . . . or from a new perspective.'

Looking beyond the cover

Identifying life events

Many factors can influence our character development; some are listed below:
- upbringing: family values, etc
- size of family, birth order, etc
- culture
- race
- religious beliefs
- first language
- places you have lived
- education: primary and secondary schools, undergraduate and graduate degrees
- major life events: moving, divorce, accidents, etc
- jobs: where, when, doing what, etc.

Try it now

You and Your Partner's Lifeline

Draw a lifeline like the one in Figure 5, showing your life from birth to the current time. As you can see from the graph there are positive and negative elements. Chart the significant events that you believe have influenced your character development, both the positives and the negatives.

- Take turns using this lifeline to discuss these important factors with your partner. When it is your turn your partner's role is to listen, without judgement, and to repeat back what he or she understood from the lifeline.
- In the same way, when your partner presents his/her lifeline, your task is not to compare experiences, but to listen and restate what you have heard.
- Capture your learnings by making a table with three headings:
  - type of experience

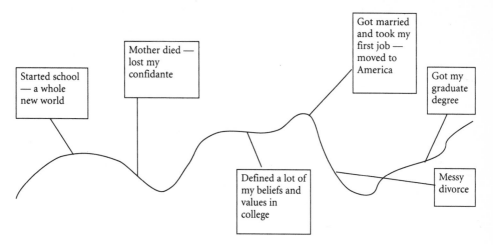

Fig. 5. Sample lifeline.

- similarities
- differences.

◆ For experiences that you think have created a common approach, list them in the similarities column with a reason as to why you think this is the case.

◆ Similarly, with experienes that might cause you to look at things differently, list them in the differences column with an explanation.

◆ Some experiences might fit into both columns.

◆ For an example of a completed exercise, see the case studies at the end of this chapter.

Understanding male/female differences

Another major area of difference between couples is the impact of male/female differences. These include both sex differences based in biology and gender differences based in society – again these two components are tightly intertwined.

According to research the differences fall into several categories:

Males	Females
◆ Males show greater visual-spatial-quantitative ability as in solving mathematical problems, reading maps, solving mazes and tracking patterns. (Influenced by society but linked to the male hormone testosterone.)	◆ Females show greater verbal ability including fluency, grammatical accuracy, written prose, verbal memory, pronunciation and verbal reasoning. (Influenced by society but linked to the female hormone oestrogen.)
◆ Men, as a result of this cerebral wiring, tend to be more aroused by pictures, videos, gadgets, and lingerie due to the visual and spatial orientation of their brains.	◆ Romance novels, soap operas, and verbal eroticism are more likely to be stimulating to a female due to her more verbally inclined brain.
◆ May appear more aggressive as aggression is linked to testosterone, the male hormone, and may have been evolutionarily selected for men to help in hunting and protection.	◆ May appear as more nurturing, as they seem to be more drawn to interpersonal relationships.
◆ Men prefer to have more space, privacy and autonomy. They are also taught to not talk about feelings as much.	◆ Women prefer closeness and report in numerous polls that they want men to talk more about their feelings and emotions.
◆ They find intimacy in working and playing side-by-side.	◆ They derive intimacy from talking face-to-face.
◆ Men have a weaker connection between the brain's two hemispheres, which can result in difficulty interpreting emotional context and non-verbal information.	◆ Women seem to read emotional context and peripheral, non-verbal information more effectively, which scientists believe is linked to the better connection of the two hemispheres of the female brain.
◆ Want to remain independent.	◆ Want to build intimacy.
◆ Report talk: men prefer to engage in communication to preserve independence or negotiate and maintain a position.	◆ Rapport talk: women tend to engage in communication to create connections and intimacy.
◆ In public men often talk more and for longer periods of time to give a 'report'. By expelling knowledge or verbally performing (stories, jokes, etc) men use communication to get and keep attention.	◆ In private settings like home and among close friends, women speak more than men to build rapport. This can be viewed by men as chitchat because there is no specific data to report.
◆ When talking about problems move into 'fix-it' mode.	◆ When talking about problems move into 'understanding' mode.

Awareness of these differing uses of communication in males and females is key in terms of respecting each other's communication styles, not being offended, and mutually flexing to meet each other's needs.

Try it now

Male/female differences

(a) Think about how the two of you view intimacy. Consider the activities you do with your close friends; do you create opportunities for both face-to-face and side-by-side intimacy? Think of one thing that you will each do to experience both types of intimacy together – and do it!

(b) To recognise the differences between public information sharing (male communication) and private conversations to create connections (female communication), think about an all-male discussion you have witnessed. Also think about an all-female discussion. What were the differences? At the next dinner party you attend, observe the conversations: what types of subjects are covered? Who leads the conversations? Discuss your observations with your partner.

Identifying personality differences

Personality differences are probably the toughest distinctions to appreciate in a relationship, as they are not directly explainable. In helping us to recognise and value these differences, temperament and loving style give us a gift.

> 'To think is to differ.'
>
> *Clarence Darrow*

Personality theory predicates that individuals possess certain patterns of behaviour that affect the way he or she is likely to respond to different situations. While these habits do not predict behaviour exactly, they can provide an indication of how individuals will approach different situations. In addition, there are no good or bad types. Your partner is not wrong, he/she is just different. We will be using the lovemate and loving styles theory to provide an objective framework to explain connections and conflicts between a couple, and look at how this affects their behaviour in relationships.

> 'I wish she wasn't so self-critical, but I'm not sure she'd be the same person if she weren't. So maybe I shouldn't wish that.'
>
> A playmate valuing the intricacies of his soulmate partner

Sources of attraction

In relationships we often appear to be attracted to those who are different from us. The attraction may arise because the other person completes us, by providing what we are lacking or long for desperately. One mindmate said about his helpmate wife, 'You will very rarely find anyone that will say anything bad about her, as she is a big time harmonizer. She is the social glue to everything she is involved with, and has a tremendous passion for getting involved in whatever it may be to do the right thing. She is an awesome mother to our children, and has an incredible, lionsized heart. She can watch the news or even listen to the radio and cry if she hears that something bad happened. She's that type of person. I love that about her.' This statement demonstrates a real love and appreciation of a helpmate for who she innately is – a solid nurturer with strong morals and the ability to harmonize. As a mindmate, these are not necessarily behaviours or values he would demonstrate, but he loved this difference his wife brought to the relationship and deeply appreciated her for it.

Additionally, sometimes people are attracted to another temperament because they reflect the beauty of their own image. Consider this helpmate describing her mindmate husband: 'What initially attracted me to (John) was a combination of things. He was good-looking and sweet. He had lots of friends that he had known for a very long time. His loyalty and commitment stood out.' While this is not devaluing him, what she appreciated was in line with her personal values: loyalty and commitment.

As you can see different lovemates are attracted to each other for a variety of reasons. These include, but are not limited to the elements described in the tables following.

Playmate connects with a . . .			
Playmate	Helpmate	Mindmate	Soulmate
◆ Together love is a never-ending adventure. ◆ Connect on a mutual love of fun. ◆ Fully appreciate each other's natural skill at tactical/tactile tasks. ◆ Speak the same concrete language and live together in the present. ◆ Share an aesthetic sense. ◆ Tune into and enjoy sensory stimulation.	◆ See the helpmate as providing the stability they lack. ◆ Appreciate the helpmate's care and nurturing when risk-taking leads to trouble. ◆ May place the helpmate on a moral pedestal - better than them. ◆ Speak the same concrete language, though their topics of interest may differ. ◆ Both share tactile interests. ◆ Will help bring out the fun side of the helpmate.	◆ Connect in their sense of pragmatism. ◆ Intrigued by the mindmate's intellectual rigour. ◆ Enjoy trying to get the mindmate to loosen up and forget about work. ◆ Admire the mindmate's ability to design cool things. ◆ Connect in their sense of freedom and autonomy. ◆ Admire the mindmate's efficiency and irreverence.	◆ Feel kinship to their romantic view of life. ◆ Feel morally uplifted by their ethical dimension. ◆ Connect in their love of possibilities. ◆ Connect in their creativity and playfulness. ◆ Share an interest in experiencing life – the playmate to have fun, the soulmate to grow. ◆ Can live the soulmate's dream.

Helpmate connects with a . . .			
Playmate	Helpmate	Mindmate	Soulmate
◆ Find the playmate's carefree spontaneity refreshing. ◆ Playmate's sense of freedom and adventure help them relax and forget about their worries. ◆ Enjoy taking care of the playmate. ◆ Swept into the now moment with the playmate. ◆ Speak the same concrete language, though their topics of interest differ. ◆ Impressed by their comfort with risk-taking, and their worry free attitude.	◆ Appreciate each other for their thankless efforts. ◆ Enjoy their mutually structured approach to life and feel secure in their mutual grounding in responsibility and duty and tradition. ◆ Put the same level of importance on experience. ◆ Speak the same concrete language and share an interest in material comforts. ◆ Set ground rules and abide by them. ◆ Live together frugally and practically.	◆ Proud of the mindmate's sober work ethic. ◆ Impressed with the, mindmate's ingenuity, as it is so different from their own read the manual method. ◆ Enjoy looking after the more absent minded mindmate. ◆ Align with the mindmate's efficiency. ◆ Appreciate the mindmate's big picture view. ◆ Share an interest in material possessions-the mindmate for status, the helpmate for ownership.	◆ Share a concern for society and morality. ◆ Impressed by the soulmate's spirituality, as it is different from their own concreteness. ◆ Find security in the moral seriousness with which the soulmate views the world. ◆ Impressed by the enthusiasm with which soulmates throw themselves into things. ◆ Appreciate the unconfined, big picture view soulmates bring to the relationship. ◆ Share a strong mutual commitment to the relationship and people.

Mindmate connects with a . . .			
Playmate	Helpmate	Mindmate	Soulmate
◆ Playmate's carefree attitude provides a respite to their intensity. ◆ Admire the playmate's ease with words. ◆ Admire the way the playmate makes things look easy. ◆ Connect in their interest in tools, though for different reasons. ◆ Admire the playmate's tactical problem solving ability in the moment. ◆ Connect in their pragmatism and admire the playmate's drive to act in the moment.	◆ Admire the helpmate's competence in caring for the home and hearth. ◆ Both value material possessions, though for different reasons. ◆ Appreciate the helpmate's ability to manage the daily necessities they would forget about. ◆ Appreciate the pleasant social life the helpmate creates. ◆ Appreciate that the helpmate reminds them of social, traditional, and familial obligations. ◆ Connect in the way they give structure to the environment.	◆ Fascinated by each other's hypotheses and discoveries. ◆ Have intense logical discussions using the same abstract language of theories, ideas and concepts. ◆ Share a love of tools and technologies. ◆ Respect each other's competence, autonomy and independence. ◆ Connect in their logical and abstract vantage points. ◆ Connect in using words as their tools.	◆ Want to help in the soulmate's growth and development. ◆ Marvel at the soulmate's depth of feeling and idealistic beliefs. ◆ Intrigued by the soulmate's insight into people and emotions. ◆ Admire the soulmate's warmth and especially the warmth they bring to the relationship. ◆ Connect in their abstract thought processes. ◆ Value the different perspective they bring to decisions.

Soulmate connects with a . . .			
Playmate	Helpmate	Mindmate	Soulmate
◆ See spirituality in playmate's artistry. ◆ Admire the playmate's sense of beauty and connect in their creativity and playfulness. ◆ Crave the playmate's content and carefree comfort with life, as it is seen as oneness with the self. ◆ Admire the playmate's freedom, sensuality and spontaneity in the real world. ◆ Swept into the now moment with the playmate. ◆ Share an interest in experiencing life — the playmate to have fun, the soulmate to grow.	◆ Make the soulmate feel safe and secure in their struggle with their identity and meaning of their existence. ◆ Calmed by the helpmate's clearcut values. ◆ Appreciate how the helpmate fufils the practical needs of daily life and makes them feel cared for. ◆ Helpmates bring the ground to their feet. ◆ Respect the helpmate's clear sense of right and wrong, which varies from their own internal struggles with issues. ◆ Connect in their people focus.	◆ See fantasy in the mindmate's ingenuity. ◆ Live together in a world of abstract ideas, theories, insight, and symbols. ◆ Admire and long for the mindmate's firm sense of identity. ◆ Admire their logical perspective, calmness and autonomy — different from their own easily upset and almost emotionally needy self. ◆ Admire the mindmate's focus — different from their own tendency to be divided. ◆ See potential and want to help develop the mindmate's ideas.	◆ See perfection in their reflection. ◆ Connect in their enjoyment of abstract communication. ◆ Have strong spiritual connection and share idealistic visions of the future. ◆ Delight in exploring each other's inner world and helping each other to develop. ◆ Share a warm and affectionate concern for each other. ◆ Share interests in growth and development individually and as a couple and want their relationship to be all it can be.

Try it now

Why are you attracted to your partner?

List some of the things that you find really attractive about your partner's personality. Think about how they are different from and similar to you and how you feel about those qualities. Consider what they bring to your relationship and how you feel about that. Your partner should do the same.

◆ Take turns sharing this information with each other.

◆ How does your understanding of temperament and loving style enhance what you value in your partner?

◆ Thank your partner for valuing your unique qualities.
We will revisit this exercise shortly.

The battle of the temperaments

> 'Sean would like Melanie to take life a little less seriously or at least not be so anxious. Melanie would like Sean to take life more seriously.'
>
> A couple describing what they wish were different about their partner turns into a battle of the temperaments between a playmate (Sean) and a soulmate (Melanie).

As our relationship with an individual develops, what we initially loved shows it has a flip side. That happy-go-lucky attitude that was so much fun becomes the frivolous, live-for-today spender. Originally we may have seen those characteristics as unique and exciting. They may have even been things we had in common with that person. For whichever reason, each lovemate can begin to irritate the other. Rather than a battle of the sexes we have a **battle of the temperaments**, where we begin to forcibly cram our partner into an ill-suited, over or undersized mould of our own seemingly perfect self. It is only when we work to understand our differences that we will be able to celebrate our diversity, rather than continually bemoan the supposed faults of others.

Battle of the Temperaments

Why don't you lighten up and be more fun?

From a playmate

Why aren't you more responsible and consistent in your actions?

From a helpmate

Why aren't you more logical and self-sufficient?

From a mindmate

Why don't you talk about what is truly meaningful and express your inner emotions more?

From a soulmate

Our mindmate earlier in the chapter noted that the one thing he would change about his partner would be '. . . to see her worry less and trust that things are going to be okay. I think she has a tendency to take everything on her shoulders like it is her personal mission to resolve. This can really affect her emotions as she feels she needs to be constantly contributing.' While earlier he really values her for getting involved emotionally and being that 'social glue', he now sees it negatively even though it results from the same helpmate qualities of nurturing and commitment that he previously praised.

The reasons different temperaments come into conflict once the 'shine' wears off in the relationship include, but are not limited to, the elements described in the table on the following page.

Playmate can conflict with a . . .			
Playmate	Helpmate	Mindmate	Soulmate
◆ Run the risk of exhausting each other with their 'Hollywood Night' lifestyle. ◆ Can blame the other for not planning for the future. ◆ Freedom with money energy and resources leads to disaster. ◆ Risk-taking causes burnout. ◆ Can be very competitive with each other and may fight for centre stage at social gatherings or compete for impact.	◆ See the helpmate's value of tradition as boring and commonplace. ◆ See the helpmate's adherence to rules and processes as dull and confining. ◆ Feel nagged by their constant shoulds and oughts. ◆ Annoyed by helpmate's righteous sense of right and wrong. ◆ May feel confined by helpmate's push for responsibility, duty and commitment.	◆ Impatient with the mindmate's need to perfect or continually improve. ◆ May feel mindmates look down on their pleasure in physical activities. ◆ May feel the mindmate dwells too long on ideas and thoughts. ◆ Don't understand the mindmate's clumsiness in the physical world. ◆ Want the mindmate to stop thinking or talking and just do it.	◆ Hemmed in by the soulmate's moral standards. ◆ See the soulmate as in the clouds and may feel the soulmate dwells on feelings and issues. ◆ Frustrated by the soulmate's talk without action. ◆ Irritated by the soulmate's constant quest for fulfillment – 'why can't you just have fun?' ◆ Uninterested in exploring their 'inner self' as the soulmate wants.

Helpmate can conflict with a . . .			
Playmate	Helpmate	Mindmate	Soulmate
◆ Frustrated with playmate's feast-or-famine spending habits. ◆ May feel playmates are irresponsible, frivolous, disorderly and childish. ◆ May feel playmates do not carry their weight in domestic duties, ◆ May get tired of cleaning up after the playmate's messes. ◆ Playmate's style may cause them to worry excessively and feel life is unstable.	◆ Routines and processes which each strongly adhere to, can clash. ◆ Can be mutually critical of each other and uninspired by similarities. ◆ Can argue over whose experience is more valid. ◆ Can grow frustrated that the other never takes a risk and appears stuck in the past. ◆ May be overly cautious together and feel that life is very conventional.	◆ Feel unappreciated when mindmate overlooks their effort to nurture. ◆ Feel that the mindmate does not pay enough attention to the practical needs of daily life. ◆ Feel the mindmate is oblivious to the feelings of others and logical analysis can be perceived as criticising. ◆ Irritated that the mindmate does not preserve and respect traditions and obligations. ◆ Focus on the future can appear to be at conflict with valuing the past.	◆ Feel soulmate may get carried away in their ideas and fantasies, compromising the family and relationship. ◆ Frustrated when their efforts to provide and nurture go unappreciated. ◆ Don't understand soulmate's push for inner awareness and soulful bonding. ◆ Discussion and activity on abstract future subjects may seem to have no substance. ◆ The helpmate may feel that the soulmate does not support their more tactile interests.

Mindmate can conflict with a . . .			
Playmate	Helpmate	Mindmate	Soulmate
◆ Disappointed by the, playmate's lack of interest in the internal word of ideas and theories. ◆ Feel frustrated with the constant need for sensory input and stimulation. ◆ May see the playmate's drive to act as impulsive and uncontrolled. ◆ May feel the playmate needs to think out actions more and consider the consequences in the future. ◆ Direct, to the point communication of the playmate can appear lacking in depth.	◆ See the helpmate's value of tradition as trivial. ◆ Hear the helpmate's reminders of obligations and should-and-ought tos as nagging. ◆ Disappointed with the helpmate's lack of interest in their abstract world of analysis and design. ◆ Irritated by the the helpmate's valuing of experience over expertise. ◆ Frustrated by the helpmate's conversations on reality and possessions versus possibility and ideas.	◆ Get very competitive about competence and knowledge. ◆ Autonomy and being wrapped up in their work may keep them apart. ◆ Can be coldly critical of each other and oblivious to the emotional needs of the relationship. ◆ Irritated that their partner never takes care of the details of day-to-day living. ◆ Feel there is no warmth in the relationship.	◆ Feel invaded by the soulmate's push for inner awareness and constant closeness. ◆ View the soulmate as emotionally needy. ◆ Frustrated that the soulmate is equally forgetful of the practical needs of the family and home. ◆ Bothered by what they see as the illogical ideas and behaviours of the soulmate. ◆ Frustrated by the gross generalizations in the soulmate's language.

Soulmate can conflict with a . . .			
Playmate	Helpmate	Mindmate	Soulmate
◆ Frustrated with their focus on the here and now instead of the future. ◆ May be offended by their loose interpretations of ethical standards. ◆ May be irritated with the playmate's disinterest in going beyond face value. ◆ May see the playmate's drive to action as hasty. ◆ May be frustrated by the lack of concern with which they live life and lack of vision.	◆ Need for conformity encroaches on their need for unique identity. ◆ Frustrated with the importance they place on status symbols and material possessions. ◆ May want the helpmate to stop living in the past and jump into the future. ◆ Irritated with the helpmate's focus on the concrete details. ◆ May get frustrated with the lack of interest in abstract ideas.	◆ Expressiveness and self-control come into conflict. ◆ Ethics and humanity come into conflict with pragmatism. ◆ See mindmate as resistant to expressing emotion and preference for what works over what is right. ◆ Can be hurt and frustrated by the mindmate's detached way of arguing. ◆ Frustrated that the soulmate is equally forgetful of the practical needs of the family and home.	◆ Can get tired with the constant 'journeys' with limited celebration of current successes. ◆ Can feel their privacy is invaded by the other always wanting to know what is going on inside. ◆ May compete on who is the 'more unique'. ◆ Can be frustrated with the other's lack of focus on the daily necessities. ◆ Irritated by the other's constant use of subjective criteria to make decisions.

Try it now

What characteristics of your partner frustrate you?

List the aspects of your partner's personality that you do not like or would change if you could.

You partner should do the same.

Now revisit the previous exercise on 'What do you find attractive about your partner?' (Page 55).

- Which of the things that you listed here as dislikes are related to likes previously?
- Which characteristics that you listed here are things you do yourself?
- How do you better understand these differences knowing about temperament and loving style?

Take turns sharing this information with each other and discussing these questions.

Functions and differences

Just as the distinct lovemates contribute to contrasting perspectives in a relationship, so do the different functions that we habitually use to gather data and make decisions. As you read the rest of this book, specifically the case studies, you will see that these differences or similarities further explain some of the challenges and strengths of a couple's relationship. Remember that even two lovemates of the same temperament may still use different functions. You might also find that your preferred functions are the same, which can lead to connection or a lack of diversity in perspective.

> 'Balance: he's wise, I'm practical. Balance: he's big picture, I'm detail.'
>
> Playmate/mindmate balance

Knowledge of these differences will deepen your appreciation and understanding of your partner, and can help reduce the judgement that we tend to place on differences. The more we can try out different functions, the more likely it is we will be able to see situations from our partner's perspective.

> 'We cover all the bases. Each of our strengths complements each other's weaknesses.'
>
> Playmate/soulmate balance

Information-gathering functions

We all use all eight functions to a greater or lesser extent, however there are two that we use with a greater ease as shown in the table on page 24. We have provided a sample simple approach for reducing the conflict from each pairing. The functions are like muscles, the more you adapt your approach the stronger the function becomes.

We have chosen this approach so that you have the tools to diagnose your relationship. Other books focus on matching each loving style with another: a written prescription, assuming a person of each loving style is exactly alike. With our approach you will gain an understanding of the interaction of your functions with the freedom to account for unique differences. Now take a look at how your preferred functions match your partner's.

Experiencing and Experiencing	Experiencing and Recalling
◆ Both partners will connect in moving outwards to take in sensory data. They will be acutely aware of what is happening in the moment in terms of the sensory environment. Both will enjoy stimulation of the senses in terms of sight, sound, taste, touch, smell, etc. Together they interpret this information to generate immediate options based on concrete reality. They will also be comfortable manoeuvring in the physical world and possibly engaging in daredevil activities. ◆ Conflict may arise if one partner's stimulation is not in line with the type of stimulation the other needs at the moment, eg one wants to play loud music while the other needs a soothing bath. ◆ Approach: practise being in tune with your partner's sensory needs as well as your own.	◆ Both partners will connect in their gathering of concrete data. Whether from the past or in the moment, both partners will want data derived from what they can see, hear, touch, taste, smell, etc. ◆ Potential conflict could arise, as the partner using recalling may need more time to process. They will want to 'go into their heads' to gather information from an internal data bank and compare it to current data. You will hear him/her say, 'In my experience . . .', whereas the partner using experiencing will be drawn out to gather information in the now moment. Using experiencing, they will see the options and possibilities in the current context and not care as much about past data. The partner using experiencing will also be more willing to take risks, while the one using recalling will be more cautious, remembering what happened last time. ◆ Approach: the partners can together practise taking calculated risks based on experience.

Experiencing and Brainstorming	Experiencing and Visioning
◆ Both partners will connect in their ability to generate options and ideas externally and in the moment and will enjoy bouncing their ideas off each other. In addition, the partner using experiencing will generate options based on concrete data and be able to visualise those possibilities better, while the partner using brainstorming will see ideas and possibilities that are more abstract. ◆ A possible conflict might occur when the partner using brainstorming draws connections and imagines ideas that the partner using experiencing thinks are a little far fetched and unsupported by the data. By contrast, the partner using brainstorming may feel that their partner is limited too much by reality and a push for action. ◆ Approach: both partners can practise working together on bringing imaginative ideas to fruition.	◆ Partners using visioning and experiencing will complement each other, as the partner using visioning will often see a complete picture of the idea and the partner using experiencing will be able to gather concrete data and see options in the moment to make it happen. ◆ Potential conflicts could arise as the partner using visioning may have difficulty putting the complete concrete data behind his/her ideas that the partner using experiencing needs. The partner using experiencing may also want to generate options in the moment, while the partner using visioning will need to step back or even walk away to process. ◆ Approach: the partner using experiencing can practise allowing time for processing and slowing down the steam of options. From there, they can combine efforts to generate concrete data to make the vision a reality.
Recalling and Recalling	**Recalling and Brainstorming**
◆ Both partners will connect in their process of pulling in to gather information from an internal data bank of facts and data gathered from experience. They will both compare this information to the present data. Both will value past experience, especially when backed by solid, concrete data. Together they can both replay their past experiences, clearly seeing, hearing, touching and feeling the scenes. ◆ They may come into conflict if their experiences differ and it may be difficult for one of them to take a risk in going with the other's information. They may also get stuck in the past, as they lack an abstract, future perspective. ◆ Approach: both partners can practise actively listening to the valid experienced perspective their partner brings.	◆ The partner using brainstorming will generate ideas and possibilities based on abstract ideas, and the partner using recalling will provide the perspective of the past to ground and support these ideas. ◆ However, the couple may also fall into conflict if the partner using recalling thinks that the ideas are too risky or have no basis in reality. The partner using brainstorming might also feel doused by doubtful comments by the partner using recalling. As the partner who uses recalling needs to process information internally the situation may be aggravated as the partner using brainstorming feels he/she is throwing out all the ideas and getting no feedback. ◆ Approach: both partners should work together to use the lessons of past experience to create new possibilities for the future. In addition, slow down to allow time to process.
Recalling and Visioning	**Brainstorming and Brainstorming**
◆ Both partners will pull in to gather information, the partner using recalling from a database of past information, the partner using visioning to unconsciously correlate and let the idea form. They will connect in	◆ Both partners will connect in their ability to bounce abstract ideas, possibilities, and connections back and forth. They will thrive, using each other as a sounding board to snowball their ideas into their full splendour.

needing time to process this information.

◆ Conflict may occur when the partner using visioning runs into difficulty putting historic evidence behind his/her ideas in order to convince the partner using recalling. The partner using visioning may also feel limited by their partner's emphasis on past experience, as they are always seeing radical and visionary new ways to try things that have never been done before.

◆ Approach: both partners can practise tracking examples of visioning that have come to fruition. These will create new data for the partner with recalling. Both partners can also practise supporting and shaping the vision with valid lessons from the past.

Both see the patterns and meanings in between the lines. They also see the connections or trends in data.

◆ Conflicts can occur however, as both parties are eager to share their ideas, they may get competitive for airtime. The two might also have difficulty grounding their ideas in enough reality to make them happen, as they lack concrete perspective. In addition, they may struggle with leaving the world of possibilities for the world of reality.

◆ Approach: both partners can practise focusing on co-operating, not competing to unlock ideas. They both can also use their 'what if' ability to analyse ideas for feasibility.

Brainstorming and Visioning	Visioning and Visioning
◆ Both partners will connect in their abstract information-gathering processes. They will enjoy sharing the world of inference versus observation. Both will construct ideas that aren't necessarily grounded in concrete reality, but are based in future possibility. ◆ Conflicts can occur when the partner using brainstorming will be full of ideas and want to sound them off the partner. At the same time, the partner using visioning may need to pull in or just not think about the data for a while until the information gels and the complete idea is generated. Both partners therefore may run into conflict over their internal *vs* external gathering of information. ◆ Approach: both partners should practise spacing the brainstorming time, so that the partner with visioning can regroup. In addition, both partners can practise using brainstorming to build on the vision.	◆ Two partners using visioning will both need time to pull back and let their ideas gel into a complete idea. They will both be willing to 'go where no man has gone before' into the future world of possibilities. ◆ Conflict may occur as they both may form their internal vision of the information over their differences in perspective. They may also have trouble explaining their ideas to each other, as their visions are internal and difficult for them to articulate clearly. ◆ Approach: both partners can attempt to make their vision more real with pictures, discussions, etc and be open to understanding the other person's picture.

Decision-making functions

> 'Sometimes I forget the value of balance, the complementary approaches. I get impatient because my partner doesn't approach tasks or decisions the way I would.'
>
> The other side of balance

Even though partners may share different information-gathering functions, more conflicts tend to occur over the use of different criteria to make decisions. 'I don't mind if you have a different perspective, but you had better make the same decision as me!' By understanding these differing processes, we are more able to comprehend our partner's point of view, and negotiate a mutual agreement.

Systematizing and systematizing	Systematizing and Analyzing
◆ Both partners will connect in moving outwards to make decisions using logical criteria to organise and structure the external world. They will share a drive for concrete accomplishment and closure in the way they live their lives. ◆ They may conflict, if they disagree on their plan of action. They may also disagree on setting boundaries in the external world, particularly when the male/female differences are added. With both partners having valuing to support systematizing, if their values system is driving them towards different decisions they may not understand their sources of difference. ◆ Approach: both partners can practise creating a written list of logical pros and cons supporting their decision and explaining these to each other to identify the similarities in approach and the objective source of differences.	◆ Both partners will connect in preferring logical criteria to make decisions. Both will gravitate towards logical data. However, then their actions may vary. ◆ Conflicts may occur when partners who use systematizing push for closure, in order to achieve goals in the external world. By contrast, partners who use analyzing will want to pull in, so as to evaluate and sort the data against their internal model. When the data is integrated, only then will they wish to take action. ◆ Approach: both partners can practise combining the external data with the internal justification to create the most logical solution.
Systematizing and Harmonizing	**Systematizing and Valuing**
◆ Both partners will connect in their need for closure in the external world. Both will push to take action and make a plan. However, the criteria they use will be very different. For the partner using harmonizing, the decision will need to be based on consensus, and one that does not cause conflict to anyone involved. For the partner using systematizing, there will be a reliance on logical data and causal effect analysis. ◆ Conflict may occur when the partner using harmonizing may think their partner is uncaring, where the partner using systematizing may view their partner as wishy-washy. ◆ Approach: both partners would benefit from valuing the external information they both	◆ If the values of both parties are in alignment, then their partner's approach can be very complementary: the partner using systematizing implements actions in alignment with an internal values systems for the partner using valuing. ◆ Conflicts may occur when the partner with systematizing pushes for closure and neglects the subjective perspective and the partner with valuing stands firm in the 'right' plan of action versus the logical one. ◆ Approach: the partner using valuing can practise assessing the accuracy of the data their partner is using and finding additional data to support their point of view. At the same time, both partners can practise voicing their criteria to the other.

bring, whether people or data focused, and being open to using both when they bring closure to a situation.

Analyzing and Harmonizing	Analyzing and Valuing
● Analyzing and harmonizing can complement each other: analyzing provides the logical independent perspective, while harmonizing can bring the balance of the group input. ● Conflicts may occur when either partner is under stress. The partner using harmonizing may become ultra sensitive to people's feelings, and omit any logical data. In the same way the partner using analyzing may make the decision without considering the group. In addition, harmonizing needs to talk through the decision with everyone, where the partner using analyzing will make a decision without consultation. ● Approach: the partner using analyzing can practise listening to the people perspective of the partner using harmonizing, while the partner using analyzing can practise voicing their rationale and being open to adapting their approach.	● Both partners share making decisions using internal criteria: analyzing through an internal categorization of data, and valuing through an internal belief system. This can mean that both partners go inwards to reflect on the correct course of action. Both are coming from deeply held perspectives: one thinks of 'what is right', the other of 'what is fair'. ● Conflicts can occur if the mental model created by the partner with analyzing is in conflict with the other person's internal values system. In the same way, conflict can also occur when the partner using valuing puts their foot down about a belief, with no apparent logical criteria to satisfy the partner who is using analyzing, which disagrees with his/her mental model. ● Approach: both partners can practise articulating their viewpoint clearly in order to make the internal thought process more visible. In addition, both partners can practise being open to their partner's point of view in order to make logical, values-based decisions.
Analyzing and Analyzing	**Harmonizing and Harmonizing**
● Both partners will go inwards to evaluate the sort data against their own mental model. The connections can occur because each partner will pause, reflect and scrutinize the data, and then support their model with logical arguments. ● The potential conflicts can appear if the resulting decisions are not in agreement, which will mean both partners have to re-evaluate their rationale. What may happen here is a competition over the logic of an argument versus a search for similarities in both. Each will see clarity in their own internal logic, until one can rework their internal model. ● Approach: both partners can practise continuing discussion on their logic and be willing to adapt their model with the addition of new data.	● Both partners will connect in wanting the decision to be amicable for each other. This normally means that the partnership is characterised by consideration for the other partner's perspective. ● This will also mean that although the relationship will be congenial, there may be hidden undercurrents that neither party is willing to have surface. This can result in passive/aggressive communication or sniping between the partners. Arguments are very stressful to both partners. ● Approach: both partners can practise using assertive communication around areas of conflict. In addition both partners should practise asking 'What do you think?' for all decisions to smooth the interaction.

Harmonizing and Valuing	Valuing and Valuing
◆ Both partners will connect in making decisions using subjective criteria: looking at the people involved, the values and the cohesiveness of the relationship. ◆ However, the partner using harmonizing will consider how everyone feels whereas the partner using valuing will ask 'How would I feel?' or 'How do I feel?' Therefore if one partner makes a decision to optimise harmony, but it goes against the internal values system of the other, it can result in a disagreement. The partner using valuing is much more likely to stand firm on their decision, if it is in alignment with their beliefs system, whereas the other partner is more likely to flex depending on what is important to the other person. ◆ Approach: both partners can practise focusing on the positive intentions each partner has around people and using empathy. Then both partners can practise coming to a solution which is amenable to both.	◆ Two partners using valuing will share a strong internal sense of right and wrong. They will both pause to reflect and may appear easy-going in the face of major decisions. In addition, they will strive to live by their internal values. ◆ Arguments can be heated as they are emotionally charged and the viewpoints are deeply held. They may connect or conflict in their inner struggle depending on the similarity of their values. When one of the partner's belief systems is at odds with the other's it can result in a fairly rigid stance, because internal decision-making processes are hard to see and harder to change. ◆ Approach: both partners can practise understanding the other's values. Based on the respect valuing has for individual perspectives they should become more open to understanding the other's viewpoint. In addition, a strong focus on life being lived by values will bring them together.

Mapping your relationship

Recognizing and celebrating your individual differences is key in creating a successful long-term relationship. In addition, you must also appreciate the entity of the couple. Mapping your relationship will help you to better understand how your two personalities come together to create a unique whole, plus the similarities and the potential differences that you might experience in the daily routines of life.

Try it now

Mapping your relationship

List your own and then your partner's profiles according to the following personality aspects:

◆ **Unique situation:** key aspects of life or your identity that shaped who you are.
◆ **Male/female differences:** key effects of sex and gender in your relationship.
◆ **Temperament:** playmate, helpmate, etc.
◆ **Information-gathering function:** experiencing, recalling, etc.
◆ **Decision-making function:** systematizing, analyzing, etc.

♦   **Direction of energy**: extroverting/introverting:

Answer the following questions to greater understand these differences/similarities.

Unique situation/male/female differences

1. How have your partner's and your own culture, ethnicity and nationality affected the way you each look at your relationship?
2. How have your life experiences, eg the family you grew up in, the relationship between your parents, or important events in your life, shaped the way you view this relationship?
3. Consider the male/female differences between the two of you in terms of gender and/or sex. How do those differences affect the way each of you views the partnership?
4. What strength and weaknesses do unique situation factors bring to your relationship?

Temperament/direction of energy

1. Look at the connection tables and think about what draws you to your partner (and vice versa). What are your areas of connection? How do you complement each other? What strengths does this bring to your partnership?
2. Look at the conflict tables and think about some of the things that your partner does that annoy you (and vice versa). Where do you conflict? How do these frustrations affect your relationship? What weaknesses does this bring to your partnership?
3. Is your flow of energy inwards or outwards? How is this similar to or different from your partner? What benefits does this bring to your relationship? What challenges could this bring to the relationship?

Functions

1. How do your respective information-gathering functions affect the way you look at data in the relationship? What strengths and weaknesses does this bring to your relationship?
2. How do your respective decision-making functions affect the way you approach decisions in the relationship? What strengths and weaknesses does this bring to your relationship?
3. Looking at you and your partner's approaches: how are they

different? How are they similar? What advantages or disadvantages could these bring to the relationship?

Plan of attack

1. How can you ensure you capitalize on the strengths of both your temperaments in the relationship? Is there one lovemate who naturally has talents in a specific area?
2. How can you overcome any challenges that you face looking at your relationship based on your temperaments? How can you compensate for 'lacking a lovemate perspective' in your relationship?
3. Based on your flow of energy, how can you ensure you both get heard? How can you ensure you give each other enough mental processing time?
4. How can you ensure that you do not over-use one temperament in your relationship?

Functions

1. Based on the information-gathering function you use, how can you ensure that you value the function your partner is using? How do you compensate for the information-gathering functions you lack?
2. Based on the decision-making functions that you use, how can you ensure that you value the function your partner is using? How do you compensate for the decision-making functions you lack? ·
3. How can you reduce the potential conflict from using different information-gathering and decision-making styles?
4. How can you 'try on' your partner's perspective in terms of the functions they use?

Celebrating the unique quality of your relationship

'We become not a melting pot but a beautiful mosaic. Different people, different beliefs, different yearnings, different hopes, different dreams.'

Jimmy Carter

Just as you cannot make your partner into something he/she is not, you cannot judge your relationship by questions about whether it looks like you thought it would or it is supposed to. You also cannot compare your relationship to another couple because you are different people with different personalities coming together. Look at your relationship as a whole, with its unique characteristics and imperfections and ask 'is it beautiful?' Embrace the differences you each bring to the whole and focus on how your relationship can evolve to benefit you both. A successful relationship is not based on a set of standards, but is judged by the fulfilment of both partners.

Try it now

Why the two of you?
Given the differences between you and your partner, why were the two of you brought together? What is the main gift you each bring to each other? What are the important lessons you can learn from each other?

Case Studies
Joan and Bill profiled their relationship using the techniques in this chapter in the following way.

Lifeline exercise
Individually Joan and Bill mapped the critical steps in their lives to date and created individual lifelines. Joan's sample lifeline is shown in Figure 6.

Similarities and differences
Joan and Bill's subsequent discussion produced the following data. They both found that this discussion was particularly helpful in clarifying their similar values, and formalising their current direction to which they had not given much concentrated thought.

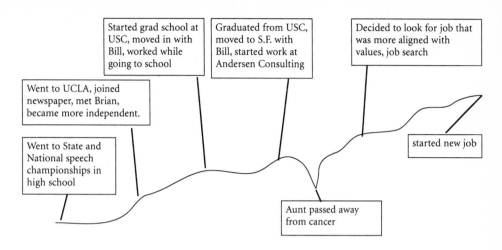

Fig. 6. Sample lifeline.

Type of experience	Similarities	Differences
Upbringing	◆ Both sets of parents are still married ◆ Both have siblings	◆ Bill is the oldest of three; Joan is the youngest of two ◆ Bill had a fairly unstable family structure while growing up – lived with a guardian from about 2–12, then with his mum and dad; Joan had a fairly stable family structure while growing up – brought up by both parents and lived in same house until moved out to go to college
Culture	◆ Both speak English as first/only language ◆ Americanized	◆ Bill's parents are immigrants from Hong Kong ◆ Joan's parents were born and raised in the US (Los Angeles)
Education	◆ Both went to college (UCLA)	◆ Bill had bad experiences in his childhood education

		◆ Joan had fairly good experiences in her childhood education; Joan has a graduate degree
Work	◆ Both are pretty ambitious in their careers. They also have very particular wants and needs career-wise; if they aren't getting those wants or needs met at a current job they will move on to other opportunities (both have had several jobs in the past few years)	◆ Bill takes more risks in his work/jobs – more willing to work for smaller, less-established companies ◆ Joan is more calculated about her career moves and deliberates over job choices – takes time off to find right job, worked at more established company to get name recognition

Male/female differences

When discussing the male/female differences Bill and Joan discovered that they shared a balance of both side-by-side activities (like cooking dinner) with face-to-face intimate conversation over dinner. In observing dinner conversations with friends, they discovered that Bill tended to be very quiet (his introverting preference) in social gatherings. He noticed that other more extroverting male friends tended to talk more about things such as sports and politics. When Joan socialized with her friends she had a few close relationships with whom she conversed about not only feelings, but also shared experiences, usually creating strong connections. Bill preferred to play video games, a good fit with the male spatial brain!

Profiling their Personalities

Personality aspect	Joan	Bill
Temperament (playmate, helpmate, etc)	Soulmate	Playmate
Information-gathering function	Brainstorming	Experiencing
Decision-making function	Valuing	Analyzing
Direction of energy (extroverting/introverting)	Introverting	Introverting

Lovemates

Bill and Joan are hard-wired very differently: Joan in her desire to have a meaning and a purpose contrasting with Bill in his need to see the immediate concrete, tangible results from his actions. However, soulmates and playmates share certain tendencies: soulmate's desire to make a difference can look very similar to playmate's need to make an impact. In addition, both lovemates read people well and can recognise when people are being honest. Playmates accomplish this through their ability to read body language cues in the moment and soulmates from their 'authenticity meter'. Both innately understand what is important to the other person (soulmate) or what the other person wants (playmate). As a result they are acutely tuned into each other, and can therefore realise any issues before they are too serious.

In their relationship, they realised that they had subconsciously divided the workload around the competence of each temperament: Bill in logistics and tactile projects around the house, with Joan managing relationships and social life. To enable them to build a stronger relationship, this profiling provided a more comprehensive picture of what they each brought to the partnership: Bill brought the concrete, now-orientation and action focus, Joan brought the abstract future possibilities perspective.

Functions

Bill used experiencing and Joan used brainstorming: the use of these functions, which both generate possibilities in the external world, were a strong connection in the partnership. In addition, Joan's use of valuing and Bill's use of analyzing were both reflective decision-making approaches. They instituted some ground rules around communication of issues that Joan felt really strongly about. If she told Bill that this was a valuing decision, he would be more careful about cross-examining her to more clearly understand her perspective. With both sharing an introverting preference they tended to process before acting, resulting in a more deliberate approach to major decisions. In profiling their entity, they realised they both tended to live in the world of exploring possibilities rather than making decisions. However, Bill's playmate temperament tended to push towards closure and action.

Valuing differences

What they valued in each other were:

- ◆ Joan values Bill's ability to provide a logical, analytical perspective, especially when her inner struggle is pulling her in many directions.
- ◆ Bill admires Joan's integrity to stand by her values.

- They both enjoy mellow time together: Joan reading, Bill programming and playing computer games.
- They both have a professional interest in e-commerce, but for very different reasons, closely linked to their temperament. Bill likes the unlimited possibilities, problem solving, programming and fast-paced style (playmate). Joan likes the ability to restructure organisations. She enjoys helping companies redesign meaningful job roles in an ever-changing landscape.
- Bill supports Joan in her quest for meaningful work.
- Joan supports Bill in his need for freedom.
- Joan and Bill balance each other with Bill's 'just try it out' approach contrasting with Joan's deliberation over possibilities.

Logan and Patricia profile their relationship

When Logan and Patricia completed the exercises they felt that the other categories had not produced many significant differences between them and therefore they decided to focus on their personality differences. They thought this would produce the biggest short-term benefit to both.

Temperament

Logan and Patricia share very different temperaments. Logan, as a mindmate, tends to live in the future and welcomes change as an opportunity to create his own destiny. Patricia, on the other hand, as a helpmate, tends to need membership and belonging. She values traditions and convention. Occasionally,

Personality aspect	Logan	Patricia
Unique situation	◆ Travelled extensively and has lived in other countries. ◆ Family is small and geographically distributed	◆ Originated in the Bay Area: has lived only in this area ◆ Very close to her family in the same location
Male/female differences	◆ Interest in watching football games at the weekend for relaxation	◆ Interest in family outings and quality one-on-one time
Temperament	◆ Mindmate	◆ Helpmate
Information-gathering function	Visioning	Recalling
Decision-making function	Systematizing	Harmonizing
Direction of energy	Extroverting	Extroverting

Logan became frustrated with the amount of time that Patricia invested in her family: she speaks to her close siblings very regularly, and he was not used to this type of frequent communication. However, there are also strong connections between helpmates and mindmates. Both like to structure the external universe: mindmates by categories and helpmates by linear processes. Both mindmates and helpmates also follow through on commitments and put structured action plans in place.

With a greater understanding of the importance of family contact to her as a playmate, they are both making an effort to manage this time: Patricia to reduce it, Logan to understand it. However, the greatest challenge in their relationship is proving to be competition and the relative absence of providing positive feedback to each other. We will review these subjects in more detail in the chapters on conflict and communication.

Functions

Again Logan and Patricia use very different functions to gather data and make decisions. Logan relies on visioning to focus on his future direction, whereas Patricia relies on recalling, with the rich data bank of sensory experiences. This can sometimes mean that Patricia is disappointed when Logan is uninterested in details, sharing no interest in decorating their house to create the homey atmosphere of her youth. However their decision-making functions, although different, have brought some strengths and challenges to their interaction. They both like closure in the external world, however they use different criteria and approaches in achieving this: Patricia focuses on people and how they will be affected, whereas Logan follows on logical data.

Valuing differences

With this data Patricia and Logan were able to view their differences from both a positive and challenging perspective, and focus on ways to value each other.

- ◆ Logan values the skills and abilities that Patricia, as a helpmate, brings such as the caring for others, the sense of responsibility, etc. He recognises that he lacks these traits and welcomes them in Patricia.
- ◆ Patricia's use of harmonizing awes Logan with the 'depth of her heart'. While he is concerned that she takes everything too personally, he sees that the positives outweigh the negatives.
- ◆ As a mindmate, harmonizing is not important to Logan. Understanding harmonizing, he realises that Patricia is not losing control when she is emotional, but that her 'decision-making function is showing!'
- ◆ In the same way Patricia realises that Logan's apparent lack of emotion does not denote a lack of caring, rather that he sees different criteria as valuable.

- Patricia values Logan's commitment and loyalty: he is up-front and clear in his promises.
- She also appreciates the adeptness that Logan brings to planning the family vacations (systematizing).
- Patricia also admires Logan's visionary determination and the ability to make real what he says he would do. _____

Discussion points

1. When you created your lifelines, what were the critical life experiences for you and your partner? How do you think those experiences have influenced your relationship for the positive? How might they have negatively affected your partnership?
2. When looking at gender differences, how easy was it to recognise report talk? What about rapport talk? Which element of male/female differences can cause the biggest challenges in your interaction? What could you do to reduce these potential conflicts?
3. What were some of the flip sides to the behaviours you valued in your partner? How will you try to recognize these differences in their good and bad forms and try to appreciate them?
4. When you mapped your different personalities, what were your main learning points? What is the greatest strength in your partnership when you look at your differences and similarities? What is the greatest challenge and what strategies will you use to address this challenge in the short-term and long-term?
5. In the exercise Why the Two of You?, what were your learning points? What was the main reason you were brought together? How can you help each other in terms of your different approaches?
6. As you move through this book, which section/chapter will be your next stop and why?

Summary

In this chapter we have identified several differences that may be present in a partnership:

- Differences in life experiences, culture, religion, education, ethnicity, etc.

- Gender and sex differences between males and females.
- Personality differences including different temperaments (driving forces) and differing ways of gathering data and making decisions.
- We have recognized that what initially may attract us can irritate us and drive us apart.
- By building an objective understanding of some of these differences, we are able to better value what each party brings to the table, and work around the potential conflicts.

In the following chapters we dedicate more content to the specific stages in the **relationship dance** (lust, limerance and attachment) and explore how knowledge of temperament and loving style can help build a sustainable long-term relationship.

CHAPTER 4

Managing the Dating Game

T he **dating game** is a crucial ritual that begins most relationships: a phase in which there are highly developed courtship behaviours and many distractions that may inhibit the selection of an appropriate mate.

In this chapter we identify many of the real and illusory factors that attract us to another person, and describe the body language exhibited during the initial interaction. In addition we show you the stages of the dating game and uncover the characteristics of different personality types in this dating scene. We do not show you where to 'find the one': this process is not like fishing! There is no place to go to catch the right person. Nor do we give you a checklist of ideal mate characteristics to bring to the bar with you. But we do show you how to understand the characteristics of different personality types in dating, so that you can relate to people better in your social interaction. Then you will be able to stop playing the dating game and start finding love.

> 'We human beings can survive the most difficult of circumstances if we are not forced to stand alone.'
>
> *On finding a partner,* James Dobson

Understanding the dating stage

Looking at the animal world, there are many strange courtship rituals and even adaptations to courtship: peacocks' tails, rams butting heads, bird dances and songs. While we don't think of our own courtship as such a colourful array of adaptation, it really is. It is a very dynamic and challenging game full of specific body language, display and ritual.

In humans the courtship rituals fall into the **dating stage**, which is most commonly characterized by **lustful love**, or physical attraction. Lustful love is the short-lived, explosive flash of passion we experience when initially attracted to someone. In the dating game we are always trying to seem appealing and attract potential mates. Perhaps this is why it becomes such a game. We try to attract rather than truly get to know a potential date. In addition, we define the dating stage as when we are searching for a mate, or when we are 'seeing' someone, but have not yet made a commitment to a dedicated, one-to-one relationship.

Loving styles and the dating game

To some of us the 'dating game' is a gut-wrenching, gruelling sport, full of bad coaching, ever changing rules and literally heartbreaking injury. For others it is a thrilling game of tactics, manoeuvring, challenges and down-for-the-count action. But no matter how we look at it, just about all of us play at one point or another. Whether we are looking for 'the one' or just out to meet people, we have to play. Knowing the theory of lovemates and loving style is very useful in helping people to discover and build a long-term relationship out of the seeming hopelessness of the dating game.

> 'There are plenty of games involved, but that's what makes dating so fun!'
>
> One perspective on the dating scene
>
> 'I think people should be less pretentious and more honest. The worst is when someone is a different person on the second date because they finally started being themselves.'
>
> Another perspective!

Factors of attraction

There are lots of theories on what attracts people to each other. Some would say we have a need to be a 'complete' person and therefore look for our opposite to complement us. Others say we are attracted to someone like us because we will potentially get along better. In reality, both are true. While both extremes do happen, most people connect as well as conflict with those they are attracted to in a number of ways. What initially brings people together can be any of a number of factors, many of which tend to actually distract rather than help us find a suitable mate.

Distracting factors

Listed in the table below are some of the factors that people cite as causing them to be attracted to another person.

Initial attraction	◆ There is a physical element in most relationships invoking a complex chemical lust. ◆ People are drawn to average features although the definition of average varies from culture to culture, resulting in varying definitions of beauty. ◆ Whatever beauty is, consumers spend billions a year in makeup and scents to enhance it.
Men attracted to women	◆ Men are most commonly attracted to young, good looking vivacious women. In evolutionary terms this trait represented health. ◆ They also seem to be attracted to women with a waist 30 per cent smaller than their hips: probably linked to childbearing ability.
Women attracted to men	◆ Women, on the other hand, are drawn to men with physical wealth: probably linked historically to economic ability to support their mate.
Lack of familiarity	◆ Our childhood playmates usually have no sexual appeal to us, as they are too familiar or fraternal.
Separation	◆ The old adage absence makes the heart grow fonder seems to hold true as being separated from a potential love interest arouses passion.
Timing	◆ If you are at a point in your life when you are longing to leave home or looking to settle down, the potential partners you come into contact with have even more appeal.
Being attracted to people like you	◆ Being attracted to people like you in terms of education, background, ethnic group and other factors is another very common factor of attraction.

Many of the facets described above are really 'distracting factors'. Though these are the features that draw us to date a person initially, dating someone solely for any of these reasons, or even a combination of them, will rarely lead to a successful relationship. There must be some depth of connection beyond physical, economical, or even the evolutionary factors of dating and mating.

Personality factors

> 'The worst thing on a date is the dead air – when you don't have anything to talk about and she isn't helping.'
>
> When you're missing that personality factor

In asking what attracts a person to a potential date, personality is the second response you most commonly hear – after physical attraction! And of course, temperament and loving styles come into play in the attracting factors around personality. We will evaluate the approach of each temperament and the contribution of each function to the dating game later in this chapter.

Lovemaps

When all the qualities a person is attracted to come together into one description, we often hear it called their 'type', eg 'he's not my type'. Sexologist John Maloney says we all develop unconscious **love maps** (or types) between the ages of 5 and 8. These love maps consist of temperamental features, like lovemate characteristics or loving style, and physiognomic features of the people around you that you chart as appealing. They also spell out other features that you associate with disturbing experiences, all creating a template or type in your mind of your likes and dislikes.

Try it now

Retracing your lovemap
While our lovemaps are formed largely at an unconscious level, surfacing this definition of your ideal mate can help clarify what you are looking for in a partner and also help you to consider if you are blocking certain people out due to unimportant or past issues.

List the characteristics of what you consider to be your type or lovemap. Consider all the attraction factors described above including physical, economic, social, personality-based, etc.

Thinking it through:
- Which of these qualities can you link to people you spent time around as a child?
- Which of these factors are distracting factors like money, education or ethnicity?
- Think about why you consider these distracting factors important and if you really should put value on them.
- Consider what you are completely unattracted to in a date. What factors from your childhood or background could cause this repulsion?
- Consider the effects of limiting yourself by not considering people who do not fall into this lovemap.

Defining the signs and signals

Once players are drawn together the game becomes filled with complex sets of signals and signs to communicate this interest that are sent by both sexes. In fact, this body language of love has been cross-culturally observed, leading one to believe that perhaps these signs are linked to humanity's common past.

Female flirtation signals

The following female body language signals cross-culturally observed include:
- lifting the eyebrows, while opening eyes wide to gaze at the other
- dropping eyelids, tilting the head down and to the side, then looking away
- covering the face with hands while laughing
- hair-tossing
- preening
- coy looks
- eye contact and smiling.

Many of these signals are seen in animal courtship as well; they most likely are evolved behaviour with some biological link.

Male flirtation signals

Males also exhibit a certain flirtatious body talk including:

- chest thrust
- tall posture
- preening
- eye contact and smiling.

It is postulated the male gestures of flirtation also have a strong biological component. Male signals are strongly linked to the dominance behaviour seen in many animal species. Not only do males try to look impressive to the female, but they also often try to intimidate other male suitors.

A smile is more than a smile

Smiling is our most diverse facial expression. Human beings cross-culturally have over 18 different ways to smile (Fisher, 1992). Exposed upper teeth characterize the *upper smile*. It shows positive intentions and signals strong interest. You'll often see this smile in the dating scene coupled with a quick raising of the eyebrows to create a flirtatious energy.

The *open smile* involves the upper and lower teeth fully exposed. This smile is a strong pick-up. Used in Eibl-Einsefeldt's female flirt or with a coy look, head-toss, or chest thrust, the open smile clearly signals interest.

Juxtaposed with these two indicators of interest is the *nervous smile*, characterized by clenched teeth and an open mouth. This would be the kind of smile you wouldn't want to see crossing your date's face, as it indicates he/she is probably just trying to survive the interaction!

Eyes are the windows to the soul

Eye contact is another potent communicator. Numerous cultures have invented the veil to avoid the aphrodisiac of a powerful meeting of the eyes. Eye contact usually produces a very strong and primitive response in our brain – either approach or retreat. If you are in a dating environment and a potential date makes eye contact, people will normally fidget a bit trying to decide what to do and then respond by either engaging in a conversation or skirting their way towards the door (Fisher, 1992).

In western cultures, where eye contact is permitted, the interested parties will often lock their eyes for up to three seconds. During this longing gaze their pupils may dilate – a sign of extreme interest. Then one of the parties will drop the eyelids and look away. Anthropologists observe this flirtatious eye contact in human as well as non-human primates and call it the 'copulatory gaze'.

> 'Perhaps it is the eye – not the heart, the genitals, or the brain – that is the initial organ of romance, for the gaze (or stare) often triggers the human smile.'
>
> Helen Fisher in the *Anatomy of Love*

Understanding the stages of the game

All of these signs and signals are actually played out in a ritual of the dating scene. Anthropologist David Givens and Timothy Peper both studied the singles bar scene in the USA and found an interesting series of protocol occurs in these venues of dating. They outlined the stages as follows:

Stage 1 – **Attention getting**

Stage 2 – **Recognition**

Stage 3 – **Talk**

Stage 4 – **Touch**

Stage 5 – **Body synchrony**.

Let's take a look at each stage in more detail.

- Stage 1 – attention getting. This stage is basically entering the bar and establishing a 'territory' alone or with your friends. Once you have your space you begin to attract attention to yourself by exaggerated body movements and louder than usual vocal cues.

- Stage 2 – recognition stage. The recognition and initial attraction begins with eye contact. When both parties are interested this is acknowledged by body language, like a smile or nod and moving into range.

- Stage 3 – talk. The talk that occurs at this stage is usually the typical bar chitchat, often with a flirtatious edge to it. What is said is not so much the key, as *how* it is said. The anthropologist Desmond Morris calls this grooming talk –

voices are higher, softer and more melodic. Tone and inflection are key. You can hide your expressions, and you can avoid certain words, but you are usually unaware of what effect your tone and inflection have on your interaction. Not only can someone make a variety of assumptions about your background, like education or geographic roots, but the way you speak also provides clues into idiosyncrasies of character, level of interest and honesty.

♦ Stage 4 – touch. Most potential dating experiences end in stage 3, before touch would even become comfortable. Before touching, body language clues like leaning in or other signs of interest usually warm the person up. This is important as touch etches a strong and immediate response in the brain, good or bad. Premature touch would definitely have a negative effect on the dating experience. Usually the female will touch first, a hand on the shoulder, wrist, etc. Whoever initiates, the receiver's response is key. A flinch will probably end the encounter as it signals disinterest or even dislike. Ignoring sends an unclear message and the initiator will usually try again. Reciprocation, on the other hand, usually means all is going very well.

♦ Stage 5 – body synchrony. Body synchrony or pacing is when two people begin to mirror each other's body language. The two pivot to face each other, lean in together, and move in sync. Even brain waves synchronize! Rhythmic movement is often linked to harmony in humans and animals.

Try it now

Working your moves

Think about the body language and dating protocol described above. What kinds of body language do you use to show attraction? You might even ask a friend or date to share their observations with you as it may be difficult to become aware of these innate actions.

Building an awareness of the signals you use can help you to send the right message in a dating environment. Look for dating opportunities where you are comfortable and can be yourself. In these environments the signals you send will be more open and natural.

As you can see our rituals of signs and signals are quite intense. We are out to attract partners under the guise of lustful love. However, are we meeting the right people while playing this game? Are we even in the right place to meet a person with whom we can have a lasting relationship?

The playing field

> 'I love bars and I love meeting people there. I just don't think they are the best places to meet a partner. Lately, the greatest success stories have come out of meeting friends of friends or family members.'
>
> A perspective on the dating scene

Every Friday and Saturday night numerous singles hit local venues to play the dating game, spending hours preparing in order to appear more attractive and drinking, or getting 'pumped up' to be more outgoing, relaxed or fun. It's time for the players to dress up, not as themselves, but as their dating personas.

> 'It seems so hard to meet a genuine person. Every guy has an act of some sort – it gets old.'
>
> A female perspective on the masquerades of the dating game

Bars, pubs and clubs, the usual field of the dating scene, are often negatively referred to as 'meat markets'. The name fits, as the loud music, a large crowd, and intoxication are not usually the best ways to help you get to know someone you would want to spend the rest of your life with. It's more likely the place to pick up on someone based on the distracting factors described earlier in the chapter. However, some individuals enjoy it for what it is: a social setting where you can meet someone you might want to get to know better in a different environment, and a fun time with your friends. Whether you enjoy the bar and club scene or not, if you want to find a serious mate in an environment where you can be yourself, it's time to widen the field.

Try it now

Opening up the field

Think about why you are interested in meeting someone special. Ask yourself: What would a lover bring to my life? What do I really want out of a relationship? What is the root experience I am seeking?

Now take out the partner aspect. How can you achieve those feelings or that root experience through other activities? If you are looking to share your life with someone, could it be a child you mentor? If you are looking for someone to explore the world with, is there a friend or even a tour you could get involved with for adventure travel?

Don't miss out on the experiences you want to have in your life while waiting for someone. What you will find is that in seeking out these experiences, you will meet others with similar interests seeking the same type of relationship.

Lovemates and dating

Snapshot of each lovemate in dating

Playmate on what he likes most about dating: 'You get to make first impressions over and over again. Not only that, but you are constantly meeting new people.'

Helpmate on her best date: 'I was taken away to Napa for the weekend. It wasn't the expense of the date (though that was very nice) it was the fact that he made all the plans. He made sure that everything was okay with me, but he made all the plans! There was no "what do you want to do?" "I don't know, what do you want to do?" '

Mindmate on a positive date: 'I like someone with their own opinion and an ability to articulate and defend it. I want someone who can force me to analyze where I'm coming from and educate me if I'm wrong.'

Soulmate on a great date: 'I want someone who is genuinely interested in what I feel, who creates a romantic environment, with meaningful interaction and who provides reciprocal feeling and acknowledgement.'

Whether we're trying to make ourselves more attractive or send the signals of interest through a crowded bar, we are rarely being true to the people we are trying to appeal to or ourselves. Due to discomfort, insecurity, or a need to be what is defined as attractive, we hide our true selves.

However, in future dates following the initial meeting you will begin to get to know the person and get glimpses of them out of their dating game uniform. Being aware of the source of these characteristics will help you to understand the people you are dating and appreciate your connections and differences.

Take a look at the table below to see characteristics of each of the lovemates in dating.

Each lovemate in the stages of dating

Type of lovemate	Characteristics
Playmate who performs	◆ View dating as an exciting game to be played ◆ Turn a date into an adventure ◆ May be the life of the party ◆ May want to do things out of the ordinary ◆ Want to experience as much freedom and variety as possible ◆ May resist settling down ◆ Enjoy the drama of a budding and/or high speed relationships ◆ When bored will disappear ◆ Drawn to people impulsively for the fun of it ◆ Stimulated by the senses of the dating environment – food, wine, perfume, etc ◆ Adapt to partners and see each one as a new and exciting experience ◆ Impress dates with extravagant gifts or expressions of affection ◆ Usually very flirtatious ◆ Sense of humour is apparent, may be very physical humour
Helpmate who honours	◆ View dating as a way to find a suitable mate ◆ Can be very formal, show respect and are usually well-mannered, punctual dates ◆ Active in socially acceptable activities ◆ Impressed by fancy dates and environments, but their frugality makes this option rare ◆ May take on the traditional old fashioned courtesy of opening doors, etc ◆ While 'proper' in public can enjoy raw jokes and discussions about sex in private ◆ Usually cautious with dates and want to fit in the dating environment ◆ Comfortable being the back-up person ◆ Sense of humour is full of a lot of 'oldies but goodies' ◆ Select traditional, material gifts

	◆ Will expect the date to participate in family celebrations
	◆ Put on a more frivolous side of themselves as it is more socially acceptable to do so when dating
	◆ May want date to be involved in their social life with friends and clubs
	◆ Sense of shoulds and oughts around what is acceptable in dating behaviour
Mindmate who challenges	◆ View dating as a strategic plan to find someone worthy of investment
	◆ Difficulty with dating – tend to be serious and cerebral
	◆ Think through relationships carefully, have strategies to get what they want
	◆ Develop a relationship as they have conceived it
	◆ Are clear with the other party as to the expectations and limits of the relationship
	◆ May have a mental list of characteristics they look for in a mate
	◆ Can view courtship as more trouble than it is worth
	◆ Society's seal of approval means little to them
	◆ Will want to talk about intellectually stimulating subjects and possibly debate issues
	◆ Will expect a good amount of autonomy in the relationship
	◆ Do not respond well to what they perceive as clingyness or over-emotionalism
	◆ Like to share ideas and theories with a date – want a good listener
	◆ Look for someone who will value their insights and ideas
	◆ Value intelligence and competence in a date, no matter what the source
Soulmate who dreams	◆ View dating as a fantasy-filled romance
	◆ Don't date – have successive relationships
	◆ Look for deep connections
	◆ Lose interest in dates that limit exploring each other beyond the surface, eg bars, parties
	◆ Want more personal and intimate dating experiences
	◆ Need to communicate with date in an imaginative, meaningful way
	◆ Breaking up can be so difficult that they will stay in relationships too long or avoid them altogether
	◆ Will put almost all their attention into the relationship when they meet a special person
	◆ Select symbolic, private and unique gifts
	◆ Love fairytale romance complete with poetry and chivalry
	◆ Blind to flaws, soulmates project their perfect image of an ideal mate onto their partner
	◆ Risk moving from relationship to relationship looking for the one
	◆ Look for uniqueness, depth and potential
	◆ Want to talk about ideas, dreams and values

Getting the most out of a date

Don't think that you can only date one lovemate. All of the temperaments can have successful relationship together. However, with each match there will be some degree of being flexible. Think about a date with each of the four temperaments. How might you have to adapt your style to fully enjoy the date with each lovemate?

Functions and dating

Recognising how functions play out in the dating game can also be helpful in getting to know someone. The table below shows you how functions appear on a date. This knowledge will allow you further insight into your date's personality and will help you to interpret and understand your interactions.

Functions in action	Looks like on a date
Experiencing	◆ In a social occasion: notices every detail, what's said, what's not said, what people are wearing, who sits next to whom and may fiddle and fidget. ◆ In any location: acutely aware of the environment and will tune into the food, music, comfort, etc. ◆ When looking at you: sees all the body language cues. May comment on specific mannerisms, the way you are dressed, the aesthetic look, etc. ◆ When talking about options for a date: provides practical suggestions about what to do now – free-thinking and flexible. ◆ On the date: very interactive and alert. Appears tuned in to you. May also get up and fiddle with stuff. ◆ Types of activities/discussions: will want to be active and may appear restless with abstract subjects or discussions without action associated with them.
Recalling	◆ In a social occasion: will appear polite and respectful of others in the group. ◆ When talking about activities for the date: will talk about what he/she has done in the past. Also will ask for information about things you have done in the past or that you enjoyed. ◆ When talking about activities for the date: may also appear cautious or overly negative about 'untried', 'frivolous' or 'expensive' ideas.

	◆ On the date: will be considerate and courteous and may appear more conventional in dress or words. ◆ Types of activities/discussion: will tend to compare and contrast data and experiences: you may hear 'better than, worse than' statements, based on judgement about what is perceived as appropriate behaviour. ◆ Types of activities/discussion: will also tend to communicate about sensory data such as gains, losses, weather, shelter, material possessions, etc.
Brainstorming	◆ In a social occasion: will ask questions and think about future focus, where current events are heading, what are the possibilities, what are the themes. ◆ In any location: may not consider practical realities and would show frustration if mentioned. ◆ When looking at you: will notice the meanings of non-verbal behaviour and will read the implications and inferences from it. ◆ When talking about possibilities for the date: will verbally explore many options, using you as a sounding board, however when polite may be reluctant to commit to one option. ◆ On the date: will consciously read between the lines and look for hidden patterns in conversation. ◆ Types of activities/discussions: discussion about ideas and concepts will be lively. May jump between seemingly unrelated topics with constant verbal brainstorming, using one idea to jump to the next.
Visioning	◆ In a social occasion: will want to discuss concepts and ideas and may talk in metaphors. ◆ May make an instant decision on a mate for life. ◆ On the date: may have a perfect picture of how the date will be, and be disappointed in the reality. ◆ Types of activities/discussion: will participate in discussion about possibilities, but then will appear to withdraw. Will then suggest a complete idea, which might appear to bear no relation to previous discussions. ◆ Types of activities/discussion: will also tend to communicate about abstract, future-focused data. Will also integrate ideas into one cohesive possibility. May not welcome questions and has difficulty describing a model in detail or explaining where the idea came from.

Functions in action	Looks like on a date
Systematizing	◆ When planning a dinner party: will focus on organizing and mobilizing the resources required to have a successful event – who is going, what needs to happen in what sequence, who is going to do what by when. ◆ When on the date: quick acting and drive for a decision and action. Will want access to logical data. Is aware of the time and attentive to time frames. ◆ Words used: will use words like 'I think', 'if this, therefore this'. May comment on what won't work. Have lengthy logical reasons for all decisions. ◆ Body language: may appear distant and lack warmth.
Analyzing	◆ When planning a dinner party: will decide on approach for the evening, what will people want to do, what to buy, who to sit next to whom, etc. ◆ When on a date: may seem critical as they challenge ideas and check data for consistency, and then comment on what is inconsistent. May appear arrogant with their ideas and not open to other activities or ideas. ◆ Words used: will want to dissect subjects to discuss a specific issue. Able to bring clarity to discussion by sorting and defining different categories. Firmly defend their ideas. Talk about their philosophies. Enjoy debating the relative merits of differing approaches. ◆ Body language: may appear distant as the external data is taken in to analyse.
Harmonizing	◆ When planning a dinner party: will want to ensure the setting is appropriate, and that people attending will be comfortable with each other. Meets, greets and welcomes. ◆ When on a date: will self-disclose to make connections with the other person and is extremely sensitive to what is perceived as conflict. High empathy skills: will know how you are feeling without you saying anything. ◆ Words used: May ask questions such as 'how do you feel?' May ask questions about what the other person wants before expressing a preference for a particular course of action. ◆ Body language: appears friendly and warm. May appear 'gushy' and effusive. Shows all feelings on the face and in the body language.

Valuing	<ul><li>When planning a dinner party: will want to ensure that no one is offended by a choice of location, food, activity, etc.</li><li>When on a date: will silently weigh ideas and information against personal value systems. Likely to be amenable to ideas yet will push back if the idea crosses their values.</li><li>Words used: will verbalize ethical issues. If they feel comfortable they may share opinions about issues that are important to them. May ask probing questions about beliefs and evaluate how they mesh with their internal values system.</li><li>Body language: may appear thoughtful as the external data is taken in to compare with their beliefs systems.</li></ul>

Try it now

Lessons learned from dating
Tune into your past and present dating experiences.
- What have you liked about them?
- What bothered you about them?
- What have you learned with each dating experience about dating and about yourself?

'I love trying new places with someone new – exploring the world. You also learn so much about yourself with every dating experience – I think (dating) is a wonderful tool for self-realization with happiness.'

Case Studies
In this case study we look at an example of each lovemate as they play the dating game. We complete the case study with a brief description of how each

Personality	Kathy	Elizabeth	Jim	Igor
Lovemate	Playmate	Helpmate	Mindmate	Soulmate
Information-gathering	Experiencing	Recalling	Brainstorming	Visioning
Decision-making	Valuing	Systematizing	Analyzing	Harmonizing
Direction of energy	Extroverting	Extroverting	Introverting	Introverting
Loving style	Extroverted improvizer	Extroverted regulator	Introverted innovator	Introverted actualizer

lovemate decided to change their approach based on the information they learned in this chapter. In the table are profiles of four different people as they play the dating game:

Factors of attraction

For all four lovemates, the overwhelming theme of initial attraction was physical good looks: no surprises there! From that point they tended to differ in their approach.

Kathy is an extroverted improvising playmate who has been married once and has been on the dating scene this time for over a year. Attractiveness tends to remain an important factor for her as she is so tuned into physical aesthetics. She also likes men who are economically sound because she values the freedom that lack of monetary concerns can provide.

Elizabeth is an extroverted regulating helpmate who is re-entering dating after having a serious boyfriend for five years. After the initial attraction, she will discount people if she perceives them to be 'playboys'. Her lovemap of her helpmate father probably helped in this process, on top of helpmates disliking unnecessary show.

Jim is an introverted innovating mindmate who is divorced and back on the dating scene. After the initial attraction he immediately gravitates towards conversation, in an attempt to assess the other person's competence. His biggest turn-off is a date who is stupid.

Igor is an introverted actualizing soulmate who has just graduated from college. After the first physical hook he is attracted to individuals with integrity who share his fascination with people: in fact he finds it hard to specify what attracts him. He tends to find something unique that interests him in most conversations, although being genuine is an important factor for him.

The signs and signals

Kathy is incredibly tuned into the physical signs and signals of the dating ritual, and once she picks them up is able to reply in the same fashion. In fact many men tend to be instantly attracted to her because of her fun sense of humour and earthy sexuality (experiencing shows!). The biggest challenge she faces is that men are often unable to distinguish her positive energy and flirtatious style from her desire to jump into bed with them!

Elizabeth recognizes the signals, and can flirt with the best of them, but the overly confident posturing of some men she simply finds annoying: she thinks that it has no substance.

Jim tends to be oblivious to some of those subtle body language signals, and either to push ahead, when the woman is not interested, or vice versa. He tends to rely on his playmate male friends to read the signals for him! Once he gets to the talking stage he feels much more confident in his ability to interest a female.

Igor feels that he subconsciously reads the signals that are being sent. He talks about impressions that he gets about people very quickly, but is often unable to back this impression up with physical data. With his empathy he also tends to be able to put himself in the other person's shoes.

Playing the dating game

Kathy in some ways thrives on the dating game. She enjoys the fact that this is a new way of meeting people, and she enjoys the social interaction. So, it's a game, that's half the fun of it! With her strong values system she cares deeply about her relationships, and is now ready to meet someone with whom she could settle down and have children. The trouble is many of the men she is attracted to and dates are also playmates and they often demonstrate a reluctance to settle down. When the relationship appears as though it is getting confining or boring, they leave! Currently she feels like she is getting burnt out in the dating scene, but is not sure why she is not finding more sustainable relationships.

Elizabeth approaches the dating game in a structured way with an internal set of standards for how it should be played. For a while she was happy with playing the field because it seemed that this was the phase she was in. Now she feels that she is ready to move onto the next stage and build a relationship, so she is consciously changing her approach.

Jim approaches the dating game with an internal strategy, and believes the end justifies the means. He doesn't particularly enjoy what he perceives to be the social trivia, but wants to find a more long-term partner. In fact he doesn't realise that, in general conversation, when he corrects the other person's word choice or debates issues with them this could be perceived as criticism or being argumentative. To him, it makes the dating seem more intellectually stimulating.

Igor tries to move the interaction as soon as possible into genuine conversation. He tries to create an environment where the other person can be herself and some of the rituals can be reduced. He tends to assess the effectiveness of the date from the extent he gets to listen and the amount the other person genuinely listens to him.

The playing fields

Kathy and her friend Amanda frequently meet guys in bars; actually she met a great guy on the street one day! She really enjoys hanging out with men with similar interests to her. She loves to ski, skate, eat great food and drink quality wine.

While Elizabeth loves to travel, and meets men frequently that way, she hates the normal dating associated with bars. She enjoys logical conversation on a wide range of subjects and finds that she is not able to find that in bars. In addition, Elizabeth has kept contact with the many people with whom she has worked over the years. Her ability to maintain these long-term relationships also provides a source of names for dates.

Jim also has initially tended to rely on bars and, while he enjoys the time with friends he finds the meaningless banter dull. He has better luck meeting people through work – he enjoys discussion around professional expertise.

Igor participates in the bar scene for its social aspect as well, though he never finds it an ideal place to really get to know someone. College has been a great place to meet people of diverse backgrounds aspiring to their dreams, and he misses this pool of interesting dates.

Approach

Each of the lovemates, based on their self-knowledge, modified their approach to dating in the following way:

- Kathy realized that she was allowing too many of the distracting factors, such as looks and earning power, to influence her decisions, rather then the personality factors that could help build a more long-term relationship. She also recognized that she was relying too much on the bar scene. She joined a roller blading club because this was of real interest to her. As a result she met men in venues other than the bar scene and had more opportunity to focus on conversational factors.

- Elizabeth began designing and making jewellery and joined an association where she met like-minded people. She found this was a more reliable way of meeting people and it also met her need to build something concrete and tangible. She became the financial secretary and found that the social events organized by and associated with this interest were a great way to meet friends and, from there, to grow the friendships into a relationship.

- Jim decided to join a debating society and a local public affairs association. He realised that by focusing on similar philosophical interests he was more likely to find a partner right for him. He felt fulfiled just by having others to discuss his theories with, which was one of the reasons he was looking for a partner. In addition, his natural scepticism and critical thinking approach would not be wrongly construed in this environment.

- Igor tended to network with his friends who often recommended people. In addition he was introduced to peer counselling, a type of one-on-one career coaching. In this way Igor fulfiled his need to self-explore and help others do the same – an experience which he could complete without a partner. He found he met many others with his interest in people there, who then introduced him to their friends. _____

Discussion points

1. How do you feel when approaching the dating game? What do you like about it? What are you irritated by?
2. When reviewing the factors that attract you to a prospective date, to what extent were they related to physical attraction? Timing? The fact that the person is just like you? To what extent were those factors related to personality? What factors were part of your lovemap?
3. What signals do you use to demonstrate attraction to another person? To what extent do you think that you are 'not you' in the dating scene? What could you do to take off this 'dating uniform' so that you could be more honest about who you are?
4. Where do you go to meet people? What are your main interests? What else could you do to meet people with similar interests?
5. To what extent are you attracted to similar types in the dating scene? What lovemate are you primarily attracted to? Why? What could you gain from a relationship with other lovemates?
6. How do the functions influence your approach to dating? How could this knowledge help you in building common ground between you and others?

Summary

- Dating is a game we all play, for better or for worse. The trick is to stop playing and be you. Lovemate and loving style theory can help you to be open to and understand the characteristics of the different people you date.
- The dating stage is marked by lustful love, or physical attraction, which is short-lived.
- Factors that distract us from what is truly important about a person include physical, economical, evolutionary and social factors. Attraction based on personality factors leads to deeper, longer-lasting relationships.
- We develop lovemaps of our ideal mate between the ages of 5 and 8. An awareness and opening up of our ideas around this

map can help us get in touch with the kind of partner we
really want.

- ◆ We all use different body language to demonstrate our
  attraction to another person. In fact, the body language and
  protocol of dating are all very complex. Each action in a dating
  environment carries a great deal of meaning.

- ◆ Look for environments beyond the bars where you can find
  fulfilment in the activities you do. Positive dating relationships
  will follow.

- ◆ Each of the lovemates and functions brings different
  characteristics to the dating scene. Learn to recognise them so
  that you can establish common ground and build a more long-
  term partnership.

CHAPTER 5

Building a Foundation in the Mating Stage

I n this chapter we discuss the **mating stage**, which is the period of time in the relationship where the couple is best suited to lay a foundation for a healthy, long-term partnership. This is the stage that causes most men's eyes to light up! Sorry guys, this chapter is not going to cover sex, a subject that is too personal, situational and private to discuss in a book about relationships. This chapter will help you and your partner create a vision, set goals, clarify values, determine how you will treat each other and clarify who does what in the daily grind.

Obviously each lovemate and loving style brings unique facets to this process, so we will clarify some of these potential differences at the end of the chapter to help you work effectively together during the process, and consider the perspectives that all personality types bring. Time spent on the exercises in this chapter can help to ensure that your partnership survives and thrives in the transition from mating to relating.

'In the early days of our relationship, when we were figuring out what we needed, wanted, and didn't want in a relationship, we agreed that our actions, choices, and decisions would first and foremost have the preservation and growth of our relationship as a first priority.'

> Be clear on what will make your relationship a success
> for the two of you

Defining the mating stage

Once you have found someone with whom you wish to pursue a more dedicated relationship, you move into a stage of infatuation with your partner which we call the mating stage. This is the period most often associated with passionate love, where your energy and focus and thoughts are almost entirely on the other person. In fact, research has shown that a person may spend as much as 85 per cent of their day ruminating on their partner. This stage is also associated with strong physical and emotional responses as neurons in our limbic system become saturated or sensitised by PEA, a natural amphetamine. This natural high can result in us being able to stay up all night, becoming full of life, feeling our heart rate speed up at the thought of our loved one, etc. Research has shown that some people become romance 'junkies', craving the high that this provides.

> 'The best time to repair the roof is when the sun is shining.'
> On creating a foundation in the mating stage

This period appears to be short-term and intense, and tends to change within two to four years to a more dedicated, long-term attachment. Many people think that the relationship is over at that point and move on to a new person. However, by clarifying the focus and direction for your relationship at this point, while you are so absorbed with each other, you will be able to create a more interdependent, sustainable relationship. Even the most

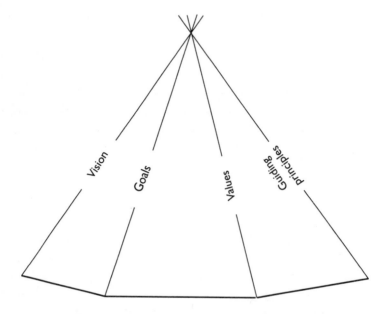

Fig. 7. The four supports provide the foundation and protect the partnership against the turbulent forces of reality.

passionate, 'meant to be' romances require focus and direction. Ultimately spending time in this arena can provide equal if not more benefits to you and your partner than just allowing the relationship to 'happen'. In addition, this process can be completed at any time in the relationship.

> 'Most couples spend more time planning a wedding than planning their lives, and get more help doing so!'
>
> On spending time laying the foundation

Writing a vision statement

To begin the process of building a foundation for the relationship you want, we will start with your picture of what that relationship looks like by creating a **vision statement**. Individually you may have a clear picture of what you want to achieve in the relationship, but couples do not often spend the time jointly defining their vision of the partnership. Creating a vision statement as a couple can be a very clarifying and motivating process that puts you both on common ground.

What is a vision statement?

A vision is defined as a picture of future greatness, a definition of core values, and a lighthouse that illuminates the path. Time and again we have seen individuals with a clear vision realise their dreams.

> 'Vision is the best manifestation of creative imagination and the primary motivation of human action. It is the ability to see beyond our present reality, to create, to invent what does not yet exist, to become what we not yet are.'
>
> *First Things First*, Steven Covey

The vision statement is intended to be inspirational and to act as a general direction statement. It serves as the guiding philosophy for the couple and helps to define the way the relationship operates, focusing attention on the future. The vision statement tends to be abstract, high level, without much concrete detail. It has also been compared to the North Star: high above, constantly present, universally known and providing direction.

Building a vision statement with your partner

Your vision must make sense to each other, stretch your imagination, and create an 'aha' effect, but at the same time be within the bounds of possibility. Your vision statement describes the grand idea of what you are about: 'Our relationship is . . .'. The purpose of your vision statement is to guide your individual and mutual decision-making, provide a yardstick to keep you on track, and provide inspiration in achieving your goals.

Creating a vision statement will take you some time to complete. Often the first ideas you come up with tend to be more detail-oriented. If this is the case you will need to continue refining the statement. It can also be interesting to approach the vision from more of a visual, hands-on approach and create a logo that represents your partnership. Consider the following example in Figure 8.

'As a partnership, we find ways to reach our individual and shared dreams, while balancing what is best for us both. We share our gifts with each other, support each other, and value our individual talents. We are one, but not the same.'

The Sun and the Moon each have their 'talents' but need each other to create a day.

Fig. 8.   Sample vision statement.

Try it now

Building your vision statement

Here are some questions that can guide you in writing your vision statement.

◆ What is our ultimate purpose?

◆ What financial results do we want?

◆ What social interactions are important to us?

◆ What mental challenges do we need?

◆ What values are important to us?

◆ What is the ultimate theme or image of our partnership?

◆ Think of the happiest you've been in your relationship. What made this time special for you?

1. Create a vision statement for your relationship.

2. Create a logo that symbolizes your vision together.

Defining joint goals

While the vision gives direction to your relationship, goals provide the concrete tangible results to define and measure what you want to achieve as a couple. Goals will help you to focus and take the steps that enable the vision of your partnership to become a reality.

> 'When we got married we talked about living and working in another country. Eleven years later, we were still in England because we had not put a target date in our intent. So we sat down together and wrote a goal: to move to America by 31 January 1987. We posted this goal all around the house. We arrived in the USA on 31 January 1987! We would still be living in England if we had not together written down such a specific goal.'
>
> Helpmate talking about a goal to emigrate to the USA

It is very important to define and write down personal goals for you as a couple: if you don't decide where you are going, you will probably end up somewhere else! There is something about writing down goals that affirms our commitment to them, and keeps them in sight and in mind. In addition, writing them down together will highlight possible areas of conflict. For instance, if one partner really wants children and the other doesn't, this is a subject that needs to be discussed and clarified.

Types of goals

> 'If we could first know where we are and whither we are tending, we could better judge what to do and how to do it.'
>
> *Abraham Lincoln*

Following are some categories for goals and questions you might consider.

◆ **Health goals:** Are you both happy with how you feel physically? Do you feel you live a healthy lifestyle? What type of exercise could you take together?

◆ **Career goals:** What do you want to achieve in your career? What does your partner want to achieve in her/his career? What potential conflicts might these goals evoke?

◆ **Family goals:** How do you define your family? What types of relationships are important for you to maintain? Do you want to have children? When? How many? What are your beliefs around raising children?

◆ **Social goals:** What social activities are important to you? How are your social interests similar or different?

◆ **Financial goals:** What income requirements do you have? What material needs and wants do you have?

◆ **Leisure-time goals:** What do you like to do in your leisure time? What do you enjoy individually? What do you enjoy together?

◆ **Spiritual goals:** What are your religious beliefs? How do you fulfil your spiritual side? What needs do you have to give back to the community?

◆ **Personal development goals:** What education, developmental or skill-based dreams do you have?

Writing goals

'We have both committed ourselves to furthering our financial life. Our goal is to be debt-free (everything except a mortgage) by 2002 so that we can afford to have children.'

Playmate talking about a goal to reduce the financial burden he and his partner brought to the marriage

Goals can be set for each partner individually, as well as for the partnership as a whole. The important thing is that they are realistic, measurable results or outcomes from your efforts, not just roles or activities. A goal should show the actual outcome expected and add substance and depth to the vision statement. Make sure you can answer the questions below for each of your goals:

☐ Who? Who is involved in the goal – one or both of you?
☐ What do you specifically desire to accomplish?
☐ Why? Why are you doing it? How does it tie into your vision statement?
☐ When? When is your deadline for accomplishment?
☐ How? Is it realistic? How are you going to get there? This statement is often not included in the main goal, but constitutes the action plan for how the goal will be achieved.

Example:

◆ Incorrect: To travel more together in the year 2001'
  This example does not tell us why the couple is aiming to travel more in 2001. Is it to experience different cultures, to rest, to shop, to see the world etc? The objective also does not state how the couple will achieve it. Will they take a vacation, take business trips together, etc? Additionally, 'in the year 2001' does not put a definite deadline on the objective.
◆ Correct: To increase our renewal quality time together, by taking a relaxing, three-week cruise by 1 September 2002.
  This is an effective objective because it answers:
  √ Who?   Both partners
  √ What?   To take a three-week leisure cruise together
  √ Why?   To have more restful quality time – and a stronger relationship

√   When?   By 1 September 2002
√   How?   DM will research options, decide location, carrier, etc.

The characteristic that gets missed the most is the 'when' element. Most people state vague terms such as 'within three months'. This is not specific enough – an actual date needs to be set, time goes quickly. If the worst happens (and only if the worst happens), preventing your success, you can reset the date, but having a D-day gives you a set-in-stone deadline to focus on.

In addition, it can be difficult to answer how something will be done. For example, if you wanted to improve communication in your relationship it may be difficult to say exactly how and what it would look like. In this case, tasks can be used to help you clarify the goal, eg type of discussions, time spent actually interacting with each other, time spent together, etc. For example, 'To improve communication by having conversations at dinner without the TV on every weeknight. (Review on 11 January 2001).' See Chapter 8 for more information.

Goals vs. tasks

Using words such as ensure, increase, reduce, obtain, achieve, attain, raise, etc in your goals ensures that the focus is on the end result and not the process.

Sample top three goals

◆ To increase our financial security by investing in property by 12 August 2001.
◆ To build a viable business together that generates our income by May 2003.
◆ To broaden our horizons by living and working together in another country by April 2004.
The 'how' will be listed separately.

Try it now

Writing your goals
With your partner, consider the categories of goals outlined on page 102 and your vision statement. Prioritize which you think are the most important and write a preliminary **goal** for each **category**.

Circle the 'who', put a box around the 'what', underline the 'why' and put brackets round the 'when' to ensure all facets of the goal are included.

While you may continue to aim for your vision for quite some time, your goals must be constantly updated to keep you on course with your vision. Celebrate each successful accomplishment!

Establishing your values and guiding principles

Your vision statement and goals give direction to your relationship, in terms of what you both want to achieve. It is equally important for couples to define their guiding principles and values, as a way of establishing the way they are committed to treating each other.

> From the beginning of our relationship, there has always been a very strong spiritual connection – I think it is because we share a lot of similar values, however, we are very different in a lot of ways as well.
>
> Importance of connecting on values

Your values

While sex and physical attraction can initially attract, similar values provide the glue that then holds the relationship together. Building an understanding of shared values is important for defining the climate of your relationship.

> 'To value something is to esteem it to be of worth. Our values drive our choices and actions: about such things as love, security, recognition, fame, etc.'
>
> *First Things First*, Stephen Covey

Examples of values include:
- achievement
- commitment
- communication

- co-operation
- empathy
- encouragement
- equality
- forgiving
- friendship
- honesty
- loyalty
- open-mindedness
- respect
- responsiveness
- sense of humour
- sharing the load.

> 'I developed values from watching families that were operating in ways I wanted to operate and reading about "optimum" family values.'
>
> Mindmate describing values

Try it now

Establishing your values

Step 1: Generate a list of the values like the one above.

Step 2: Each partner should note his or her top five values.

Step 3: Each person should explain why they chose each value and what it means to them. Without being confrontational, ask several situational questions to your partner to help clarify the value. For example, if your partner chose honesty you might ask a question like, 'If you were in a store and the clerk gave you an extra £20 in change by mistake what would you do?' Books such as Gregory Stock's *Book of Questions* can also help to clarify how you each put your values into action.

Step 4: As a couple, decide on the values that are most important to the two of you and define them in your own words.

Guiding principles

Guiding principles are the standards each partner agrees on, in order to manage their interactions. They can be fairly obvious and easy to set, but more difficult to maintain within day-to-day interaction. The purpose of these guidelines is to provide a common approach or structure for managing the relationship, so that the couple is not always tied up doing damage control. Obviously there is no need to create such a behavioural code around every aspect of your interaction. Guiding principles are normally set for areas where conflict arises, but these areas will vary from couple to couple. They could include watching TV, communication, quality time, personal time, or handling stress or activities that neither of you like to do. Examples of categories and questions to consider are listed below:

Conflict situations:
- What is the protocol you practise for listening?
- What is the appropriate manner of communication, eg tone of voice, volume, etc?
- How do you clarify and ensure understanding?
- How do you handle anger and other emotions?

Watching TV:
- How much TV will be watched on weeknights and weekends?
- How will you decide which programmes to watch?

Making decisions:
- What will you make decisions on mutually versus separately?
- What is your decision-making process?

Managing time:
- How will you decide to spend your time at the weekends?
- How much quality time will you spend together per week?
- How will you correlate your schedules?
- How will you balance time with friends, family, just the two of you, etc?

Try it now:

Compile a list of your joint guiding principles.

Managing reality

> 'I think what I've noticed is that our roles tend to take the
> form(s) most favourable for achieving balance. For example,
> one of us takes the role of "homemaker" if the other is
> particularly involved in a big project at work. This flip-flops
> depending upon which one of us is engrossed in work.'
>
> Harmonizing amid the realities of daily life

While it is beneficial to envision your ideal world, most of us
become submerged in the detailed realities of daily living. Life
would be wonderful if we could live constantly in the sunshine of
our love, but as the dishes won't wash themselves and the children
can't be beamed home from school, we must deal with more
mundane tasks as well. Spending time identifying who prefers
which chores can soothe the day-to-day stresses of a relationship
and avoid long-term conflicts. Research has shown that women,
on average, still carry the majority of the burden of household
and family activities, even if they are working full-time. In today's
'partnership relationships', where equality of partners is the
driving force (versus economic partnerships in previous ages,
where the money-earner was in the position of power) it is
important to balance the workload, so that the resultant time can
be spent together on quality activities.

> 'I am the repairman and she is the wealthy socialite. I water the
> plants, she feeds the cat. I blow leaves, she cleans up after the
> cat, I wash dishes, she makes them dirty.'
>
> A playmate's more flippant approach to dividing tasks!

Think about the daily tasks which consume our lives; this list
includes such things as:

- managing the finances
- laundry/ironing
- house maintenance
- shopping
- cleaning and tidying
- entertaining

- managing the garden
- organizing family celebrations
- cooking and washing up.

If you have children, this creates an additional list including such things as:

- managing homework
- driving to swimming, sports, other interests
- clothes shopping
- outings with children.

> 'We allocate household responsibilities based on who likes to do what, who hates to do what, and who can tolerate it. For instance, he looks after the car because he understands it. I look after the meals for special events because I enjoy it.'
>
> Playmate talking about allocation of tasks with her mindmate partner

Try it now

Managing reality

Task	Who	Time	Pleasantness	Alternatives

1. Using the headings above, with your partner list all the household, family maintenance and parenting tasks you can think of. Look at the three columns entitled 'who', 'amount of time', and 'pleasantness'.
2. For each activity fill in who does it and the amount of time it takes.
3. Then have each person put their own pleasantness ranking on the task (1 = gross, 5 = enjoyable).
4. Based on differing pleasantness rating and amount of time each activity takes, are the household tasks divided fairly?
5. How else could you allocate who does what?

Working towards the best possible division of labour will make the mundane more bearable.

Lovemates and loving styles in the mating stage

> ### Lovemate snapshots on mating
>
> A playmate and soulmate approaching laying a foundation:
> 'John is really big on voicing his dreams and aspirations for the
> future. He wants to be doing his life's dream in a few years and he
> really wants me to think big about the future. My life is going
> extremely well right now and I don't get the big bang out of the
> future dream scenario that he does. I'm constantly reshaping my
> life, and I'm doing the work that I really love. I'll deal with the
> future when I get there.'
>
> A helpmate describing how her family values were developed:
> 'We decided on our family values together. We sat down and
> wrote out what was important to both of us.'
>
> A mindmate describing how his family values developed:
> 'From watching families that were operating in ways I wanted to
> operate. Reading about "optimum family values" over time.
> Making great mistakes in family situations that caused pain to
> myself and others.'

Each lovemate approaches the mating stage in differing ways as
you can see in the table below. The more collaborative
temperaments (soulmates and helpmates) may gravitate more
towards activities such as defining vision, values and guiding
principles. The more pragmatic temperaments (playmates and
mindmates) will tend to have more interest in outcomes versus
the process.

	Strengths	Possible challenges
Playmate	◆ Bring a clear, realistic perspective of the current situation. ◆ Move to action in accomplishing goals. ◆ See lots of options for the couple. ◆ Easy-going approach to major goals that could dramatically affect the couple. ◆ Help to clarify values through situational questioning. ◆ Seek fun and enjoyment as the foundation of the relationship.	◆ May think defining a vision is a waste of time. Will prefer goals, as they are more action-oriented. ◆ May think more of current tactics and details versus long-term direction. ◆ May find it difficult to define values (particularly crafting playmates) - they are affected by the situation. ◆ May not want to be 'confined' by guiding principles. ◆ May not have the patience for talking about it - would rather do it.

Helpmate	• Will focus on the practicalities of life such as setting goals and defining guiding principles. • Will adopt a structured step-by-step approach to setting goals: naturally define outcomes and work towards them. • Value guiding principles so they know the process. • Seek stability in the foundation of the relationships. • Demonstrate strong loyalty to the relationship. • Bring hard work, dedication and follow through as values.	• May be held back from future possibilities if they do not have any concrete historic experience. • May view the vision statement as impractical. • May be too task versus possibility focused. • May take on many responsibilities, but then feel abused. • If responsibilities are not adhered to may go into blame and complain mode.
Mindmate	• Naturally focus on future strategic possibilities. • Able to easily categorize goals and activities. • Will be able to critically evaluate and sort through different options. • Will be able to critically consider each value and its definition. • Seek efficiency and ideal operation of the relationship. • Will enjoy defining their own destiny.	• May not be realistic regarding what can be achieved. • May resist the 'menial' tasks of the home. • May be overly critical and oblivious to his/her partner's feelings in developing the foundation. • May be too determined in achieving their own goals to balance with their partner's needs. • May agree with guiding principles but miss the implementation at the moment of interaction.
Soulmate	• Will view setting goals and creating a vision as an opportunity to grow and learn together. • Will want to define values and ensure they are meaningful to both partners. • Will want to focus guiding principles around relationships and communicating, not around concrete tasks and activities. • Seek growth and togetherness as the foundation of the relationship. • Are creative and future focused in identifying direction. • Constantly re-evaluate their own and their partner's search for self.	• May have difficulty being specific enough in goals and guiding principles. • May be unrealistic and reluctant to delve into details. • May appear too focused on the vision and the goals versus the realities of life. • May appear reluctant to give up 'their cause' for the benefit of the relationship. • Rarely stop to celebrate accomplishments but drive on in their journey through life.

As you can see, different lovemates bring a diverse array of strengths and challenges to the mating stage. For example, if a soulmate enjoys the abstract definition of vision in the future and her partner lives in the past (helpmate), the two may appear to be at cross purposes, even though they are both committed to each other and the relationship.

Understanding these differences is key in working together to build a solid foundation.

Functions in the mating stage

The addition of partners using differing functions can also influence the process of defining direction. Remember that the temperaments use the functions most easily, as shown in the table in Chapter 2.

Strengths and Challenges of Functions in Mating Stage		
	Strengths	**Weaknesses**
Experiencing	* Great at improvizing options for current reality. ♦ Now-focused, action-oriented - want to make the goals happen now. ♦ Want visions to be attention-grabbing. ♦ May feel they can handle the future risks, little fear. ♦ Ready for a challenge.	♦ May only focus on the here and now. ♦ May change direction too frequently. ♦ May have difficulty focusing on the future. ♦ May get bored just talking about it. ♦ May jump ahead in the process.
Recalling	♦ Bring a historical perspective to goals and planning. ♦ Bring an organized, sequential thought process. ♦ Want to maintain any traditions from previous relationships that have worked. ♦ Ability to organize what has to be done in an orderly manner. ♦ Want to plan for contingencies in the relationships.	♦ May get stuck in the details. ♦ May not respond positively to new ideas and change. ♦ Want practical applications, may be impatient with the abstract. ♦ May be resistant to ideas they see as unrealistic. ♦ May bring forward old failures – 'We can't do that because . . .'.
Brainstorming	♦ See lots of options with little perspective on limitations. ♦ Future focus and big-picture	♦ May have trouble narrowing down the vision statement and focusing on goals: no limitations.

	ability is critical for defining vision. ◆ Have a fresh perspective - will look at things from new angles and encourage different perspectives. ◆ Ability to identify trends and patterns in how factors relate to each other. ◆ Flexible and encouraging of ideas.	◆ Try to take on too many ideas and have difficulty prioritizing between multiple ideas. ◆ Ideas might not always be grounded in feasible reality. ◆ May not see the down side when excited about ideas and possibilities. ◆ May not consider pratical details.
Visioning	◆ Develop completely new ways of approaching a relationship. ◆ Insightful vision of the future with a broad, long-range perspective. ◆ See the deeper meaning and implications. ◆ Have a complete vision of what they want the relationship to look like and of how it will all work out. ◆ Bring an independent perspective.	◆ May be unable to articulate the vision or involve their partner in their vision. ◆ May not be willing to listen to other ideas that are not in agreement with their vision. ◆ Their vision may appear completely unrelated to current data. ◆ The drive to achieve the vision without compromise may result in a rigidity of approach. ◆ Limited awareness of concrete details.
Systematizing	◆ Emphasize logic and equality in establishing who does what. ◆ Analyze values using logical approach. ◆ Want the process to be effective and serious. ◆ Provide detailed, logical support for all opinions. ◆ Gifted in categorization and definition of goals.	◆ May be impatient in delayed decision-making - may push for closure too quickly. ◆ Systematic approach may not take into consideration the people aspects. ◆ May appear uncaring in the process with their partner. ◆ Point out inconsistencies and inaccuracies in reasoning. ◆ May appear critical.
Analyzing	◆ Logical and analytical approach to establishing vision and goals. ◆ Enjoy creating new hypotheses and frameworks for functioning in the relationship. ◆ Push for consistency in the	◆ If the information does not map with their current model, they will challenge the data and approach. ◆ May question the values exercise as to how much values affect the

	whole result. ♦ Enjoy the analysis - search for the principles behind the problems. ♦ Will analyze data and be able to present an alternative viewpoint.	quality of a relationship. ♦ The logic they give for managing reality may be based on their own internal logic. ♦ May appear to be overly argumentative about specific data. ♦ May not even identify with the term values (particularly crafting (playmates).
Harmonizing	♦ Sensitive to their partner's needs in all aspects of building a foundation. ♦ Push for consensus on ideas. ♦ Place high importance on guiding principles and establishing norms of behaviour. ♦ Quick to point out strengths and make the partner feel good about him/herself. ♦ Comfortable with self-disclosure around emotional issues.	♦ Feel uncomfortable when conflict erupts and may not want to move on without resolution. ♦ May not reveal what they really want to do with the push for consensus and then go into passive aggressive behaviour. ♦ Showing emotion on the face can be unproductive at times. ♦ May have an unconscious list of shoulds and ought-tos. ♦ May get annoyed if appropriate behaviour is not demonstrated.
Valuing	♦ Have strong beliefs about the way the relationship should work. ♦ Highly value their partner's different perspectives. ♦ Place high import on values exercise. ♦ Seek a vision that adheres to their beliefs. ♦ See the uniqueness of their partner separate from themselves.	♦ May adamantly oppose ideas that go against their internal values system. ♦ May refuse to compromise values to take advantage of alternative solutions. ♦ May be judgemental when values aren't in alignment. ♦ May appear unrealistic in ideals and may be reluctant to accept logical arguments that go against beliefs.

Case Studies

In this case study we look at two couples as they lay the foundation in the mating stage. They used similar steps, but approached them very differently based on their temperament and loving style. The profiles of the two couples are on the next page.

Personality	William and Mary		Robert and Anne	
Lovemate	*Helpmate*	*Helpmate*	*Mindmate*	*Soulmate*
Information-gathering	Recalling	Recalling	Brainstorming	Brainstorming
Decision-making	Systematizing	Harmonizing	Analyzing	Valuing
Direction of energy	Introverting	Introverting	Introverting	Introverting
Loving style	Introverted regulator	Introverted nurturer	Introverted innovator	Introverted advocate

Approach to the mating stage

Both couples approached the mating stage with their eyes wide open. William and Mary placed great emphasis on this stage for several reasons:

1. Mary had come from a broken home and did not want to relive that experience with her own family.
2. The church they were members of organised a series of workshops that couples who were considering marriage had to complete.

Robert and Anne were committed to the process because they had both been divorced and they did not want to repeat the process. As Robert said, 'the courtship ritual is like the dance of the seven veils: I want to make sure we remove the seventh veil before we get married so there are no surprises!' 'Both couples *consciously* focused on creating a foundation upon which to build their long-term relationship.

Vision

William and Mary did not start with a vision statement, they began with the more tactical steps such as answering some of those difficult questions around a relationship: children, religion, contraception, etc. Helpmates tend to start with the concrete issues to build to the more abstract vision. Robert and Anne, on the other hand, created an overarching theme for their relationship. They did not specifically label this as a vision statement, but it certainly acted as a guide to them in making decisions: they wanted freedom so that they could pursue choices as a couple. This approach is not surprising considering both partners use brainstorming.

After attending a couple's workshop, both couples formalised their vision statement and logo, as seen in Figures 9 and 10.

'*We are an everlasting partnership based in support and fun where each of us inspires the other to grow individually and together.*'

William and Mary's logo that symbolizes their mission together:

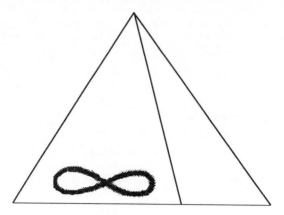

The pyramid symbolizes a solid foundation building towards infinity.

Fig. 9.   Sample vision statement and logo.

Goals

Both couples have defined numerous goals for themselves over time. Their financial goals serve as a good example.

William and Mary defined clear financial goals for themselves. These goals were concrete deliverables to help support living life by their values. For instance:

◆ To support achievement: to purchase our first home by 31 December 1999.
◆ To support education: by December 2000 to save enough money for both children's college education.

Robert and Anne defined their financial goals by checking how they aligned with their vision statement. For instance, to reduce their financial burden and enable them to have more time together away from work:

◆ They financed their house on one income.
◆ They bought a less expensive car.

As you can see, William and Mary's goals were based on specific economic outcomes, Robert and Anne's were based on lifestyle choices.

'*We believe in supporting our individual soul growth and growth as a couple.*'
Robert and Anne's logo that symbolizes their mission together:

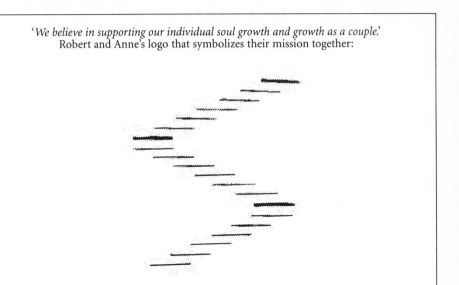

Climbing stairs to a new level and discovering the journey continues in a different direction.

Fig. 10. Sample vision statement and logo.

Values

Both couples defined values for their relationship, but in very different ways.

When William and Mary were dating, they became conscious of each others' values by observing behaviours. How clean did she keep her car? What type of things did she like to do? How did she treat others? As their relationship developed, they realized that they shared similar values and they therefore combined the values from both family backgrounds. When they started a family, they realized the need to write down these beliefs, so that they could share them in a formal manner with their children. They listed the values as shown below:

- ◆ supportive family
- ◆ compassion
- ◆ education
- ◆ religion
- ◆ health
- ◆ achievement
- ◆ open-mindedness
- ◆ courtesy
- ◆ teamwork
- ◆ freedom
- ◆ honesty.

Each value was defined, and the values were stuck up throughout the house to keep them in sight and in mind.

By contrast, Robert and Anne were aware of each other's values, but indicated this more through general statements than specific observations. They later found a quotation that seemed to capture the essence of the values they wanted to define their interaction with each other. They had this needlepoint created and hung in the kitchen for easy reference. _____

> 'Oh. The comfort – the inexpressible comfort of feeling safe with a person – neither having to weigh thoughts nor measure words, but to pour them out, just as they are, chaff and grain together, knowing that a faithful hand will take and sift them, keep what is worth keeping, and with a breath of kindness blow the rest away.'

Guiding principles

William and Mary spent very little time defining guiding principles, instead relying on the clear definition of roles and responsibilities to guide their daily actions. By contrast, Robert and Anne focused almost immediately on the guiding principles they needed to establish to make the relationship work, while placing a much-reduced emphasis on specific roles and responsibilities. This is what you might expect based on the fact that William and Mary were more concrete and Robert and Anne more abstract.

The guiding principles that Robert and Anne established are:

◆ When communicating there will be no second-guessing and no games. We started with a friendship, and we want to sustain that even if the 'romance' doesn't last. (Established in the first week of the courting relationship.)

◆ We are not going to climb the corporate ladder, but instead focus on living our lives together.

◆ We are not going to have more children (they each had children with their previous partners).

◆ We will have a relationship where we both want each other, but are not dependent on each other.

◆ When making decisions we will not always make them together, but we will consider the impact on the relationship when making the decision.

All these principles were defined within six months of being a couple and proved to be invaluable in smoothing any uncertain paths.

Roles and responsibilities

William and Mary jointly decided on the daily allocation of family responsibilities based on proficiency and the degree to which they enjoyed the task. It was important to them that they both pulled their own weight. For instance:

- Mary planted flowers because she liked to see things grow.
- William cut the hedges: he liked the garden to look neat (systematizing).
- Mary dusted because she had allergies and this had to be completed on a regular basis.
- William washed the cars because he was taller and they owned a 'high' car.
- Mary liked doing the laundry.
- William liked fixing things.

Robert and Anne tended be flexible around household activities depending on who was more busy: 'we have no his or her responsibilities, whoever gets to the responsibility first does it.' They were comfortable with the lack of formalized structure.

Discussion points

1. What stage is your relationship in? To what extent are you experiencing intrusive thinking? Emotional highs? How do you feel about this? How would you react if the relationship were to move onto a more even keel?
2. How successful were you in defining the vision for your partnership? What were your learning points as you discussed the subject together? How do you think time spent in this area will benefit your relationship?
3. What type of personal goals did you define for yourself and your partner? What conflicts were there in the goals that you listed? How did you resolve these conflicts? How did it help you to write down these goals?
4. When defining your values, to what extent were those you each selected similar? How were they different? How will understanding these values build a strong foundation in your relationship?
5. When you discussed managing reality, what happened? What tasks or activities appeared to be divided unfairly? How did you resolve these differences?
6. How did you discover your temperament influenced your approach to laying the foundation in your relationship? What

challenges did this bring? To what extent were your approaches similar?

7. How did the functions you use for information-gathering and decision-making influence the process? To what extent were you able to use other functions or understand your partner's approach?

8. Which of these activities had you already begun in your relationship? Which were new activities? What do you perceive to be the benefit of using these techniques to build a solid foundation for your partnership?

Summary

In this chapter we have highlighted the importance of laying the foundation for your relationship in the mating stage, when you are still absorbed with each other. To do this you need to:

♦ Define a vision for your partnership that captures the essence of your direction and provides a yardstick for making mutual decisions.

♦ Define specific goals for your life that will provide the concrete measurable outcomes to which you are both committed.

♦ Establish values and guiding principles to create the interaction climate between the two of you.

♦ Finally, provide your relationship with the reality check, by listing and evaluating who does what in the basic tasks around managing the logistical aspects of living together.

Our temperaments and the functions we use to gather information and make decisions influence each of these activities. By approaching the mating process with this information as a backdrop we can better create a solid grounding on which to build the long-term relationship.

CHAPTER 6

Relating: Communicating with Your Mate

Congratulations if you have made it to the **relating** stage: so there's good news and bad news! The good news is that you have made the difficult transition from mating to relating, the toughest change. The bad news is that there will be constant hard work ahead. The good news from that is that the exercises, tools and techniques in the next three chapters will help guide you through the tough times, and enhance your enjoyment of the good times as well. And the output is definitely worth the input.

Defining the relating stage

For the **relating phase** we have concentrated on the aspects of a relationship that most influence a successful long-term partnership:

- ◆ **Communication:** the critical component facilitates most of your interaction.
- ◆ **Managing conflict:** an area where the relationship is built or destroyed.
- ◆ **Spending quality time together:** a key factor, which provides the energy and growth required to sustain companionship.

So read on, and good luck building or rejuvenating your relationship.

> 'The foundation of our relationship is commitment. Sometimes when we are mad, the love isn't enough and that is when our commitment kicks in.'
>
> Helpmate on tough times

Communicating

Effective communication between partners plays a fundamental role in building a productive relationship. Making decisions, understanding our partner's wants and needs, listening to our partner's point of view, planning time together, discussing finances, resolving conflict are all examples of communication in action. Yet despite the amount of time we spend communicating (as much as 90 per cent of our day!), many of us give little thought to the complexity of the process and the opportunities for our interaction to go awry. To make the situation more complex, we also tend to speak and process data in the language of our temperament, with the result that we appear to be talking at cross-purposes.

In this first chapter in the 'relating' section we begin by focusing on the communication process between you and your partner, and provide tools and techniques for improving communication effectiveness in every facet of your relationship. Although many of the principles and techniques described in this chapter may seem to be nothing more than common sense, as we all know common sense is not necessarily common practice!

> 'I'd rather spend time with him than with anyone; the chemistry is good, the energy is good. This is the way life is supposed to be.'
>
> Playmate on good times

What is communication?

> 'We talk, but how often do we communicate?'

Communication is critical to building a long-term relationship and is often hailed as the solution to marital discord. Yet we take communication for granted: we think we know how to communicate, but do we really? Many of us are more concerned with talking or 'scoring points' rather than really understanding our partner's perspective. In this section we are going to go back to zero, in order to provide a model that will not only help you better comprehend the process, but also show you how to use communication tools and techniques to raise your communication effectiveness with your partner.

Defining communication

Communication is defined as the exchange of information between sender and receiver.

> 'Speech is a joint game between the talker and the listener against the voices of confusion.'
>
> *The Human Use of Being – Cybernetics and Society,*
> Norbert Weiner

In order for communication to be effective, the message must be clear and the receiver must receive it, process it and act on it. Communication includes the words said, the way they are said and the body language used during the process.

Building the communication process

Normally when people are asked to identify the beginning of the communication process they say it begins with words or by getting the other person's attention. In reality, the communication process is more complex than that. In working with individuals

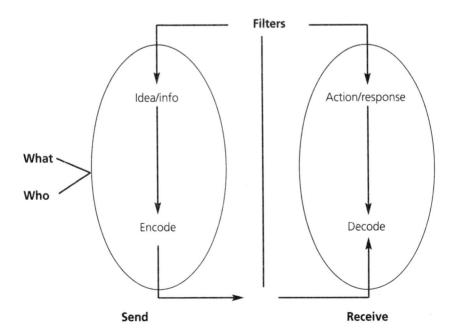

Fig. 11. The communication process.

and couples, we have found that the use of a model to clarify steps in the process is helpful.

Sending the message

As you can see in Figure 11 the process begins when the sender has an idea, thought or information that they wish to communicate. The sender then must formulate or organise the information considering not only who will be the receiver, but what they wish to achieve as a result of sending the message. When the information has been mentally prepared, it is ready to be sent.

When we are communicating with another person face-to-face, we use both verbal and non-verbal communication. Verbal communication refers to the actual *words we use* (word choice/dialogue), and the *way we say the words* (tone, pitch and volume). Non-verbal communication refers to *body language* (expressions, gestures and posture). When we communicate with someone with whom we have an ongoing relationship, like our partner, credibility also plays a role. Credibility usually comes from the amount of connection, knowledge or reliability we recognise in the communicator. On a first meeting body language is the main component of communication. As we saw in the dating chapter, much of our initial impressions of our partner are based on a complex series of 'flirting' body language cues. When we have known someone for a while, credibility becomes the most important factor.

Receiving the message

When we send a message, if we're lucky the other person will receive it. However, too often filters such as bias, insufficient interest, rehearsing, lack of understanding and distraction prevent the listener from receiving the message. If the listener does receive the message, they then process it against their own reference bank and decode it appropriately in order to take action or provide a response.

Complexity of the process

Figure 11 represents a simple explanation of the communication process. All the steps actually happen simultaneously. As the sender is thinking of an idea, they are formulating a sentence and possibly already sending the message. On the other end the receiver is sending back a complex combination of responses during the whole transmission, while at the same time processing and decoding the information.

Lots of things can go wrong in this process when communicating with our partner. You may have an irrational idea, or so it appears to your partner! You may structure the information erroneously for them: too long-winded, too direct, etc. By using the wrong words (too complex, non-precise), you could also bore or irritate him/her. In addition, you might not deliver the words effectively (negative emotion influencing your tone and body language). From the other side, your partner might filter out the message or interpret it incorrectly because of their different frame of reference. Then, they might provide a completely inappropriate response. The process is so complex that it is amazing anything is communicated accurately at all!

Personality differences will also drastically affect the entire communication process. Each lovemate values distinct ideas, will organize data in varying ways, select unique words and use different intonations and body language cues. We will examine these languages in more detail later in the chapter.

Sending the message

The words we use

> 'I could probably be more specific in what I communicate. I think I sometimes might not come right out and say it first and this can frustrate my partner because he is a pretty straightforward person.'
> Soulmate talking about word choice with a playmate

While the actual words we use represent only 7 per cent of the communication process, word choice is still something to carefully consider. Many relationships have words or phrases that activate 'hot buttons'. 'You're just like your mother' might be considered as one!

Some important points to remember about the words that you use when communicating with your partner are:

◆ If you are trying to make a point with your partner, be careful with the word 'but': it tends to disqualify all other words used previously in the sentence. For instance 'I understand you are really busy right now *but* I need your help' actually negates the beginning of the sentence and says I don't care about how busy you are, I am too! The word *however* is much better as a bridging word.

◆ When communicating about feelings use 'I' messages. Instead of saying 'You made me feel . . .', say 'I feel'. This makes the focus of the message be you instead of them and is less accusatory.

◆ Be aware of the 'taboo' words or subjects in your relationship that cause you or your partner to see red and try to avoid using these words, particularly in a stressful situation.

◆ Watch words that tend to over-generalise actions: 'you never do this', 'you always'. These words will tend to escalate a negative situation.

The four lovemate languages

To make word selection even more complex, each lovemate will speak its own language as shown in the table below.

Communication component	Playmate	Helpmate	Mindmate	Soulmate
Type of language	◆ Colloquial: current jargon, irreverent words and phrases	◆ Conventional: respectful, language of the group	◆ Precise: exactly the right word to describe the nuance of a situation	◆ Global: 'larger than life' words with hyperbole
Structure of words	◆ Concise: less is more	◆ Detailed: start at the beginning and work through a step at a time	◆ Word arsenal resulting in long, complex, logically deductive sentences	◆ Long, flowing sentences with general statements and multiple ideas interwoven
Abstract/concrete	◆ Concrete: what is observable in the tangible	◆ Concrete: particulars in material or social surroundings	◆ Abstract: concepts, trends, future possibilities with logical data	◆ Abstract: impressions, ideas and feelings with a relative

				inability to quote supporting concrete data
Conversations about	◆ Literal rather than figurative ◆ Details and devoid of planning ◆ Specific rather than general ◆ Do it rather than talk about it	◆ Solid sensible topics, past experience and better than, worse than ratings: food, clothing, credits, debits, prices, wages, gains, losses, recreation, weather, shelter, rich/poor, accidents, disasters, saving money	◆ Taking information and going straight to possibilities ◆ Things that are not necessarily tangible ◆ The future ◆ Abstract ideas-little discussion on details	◆ Future pictures ◆ Metaphors and similes ◆ From a few particulars to sweeping generalizations
Starting point	◆ What's easiest: parts to whole	◆ What's first: parts to whole	◆ What's the big picture and the major categories: whole to parts	◆ An idea immediately going to the big picture
Style	◆ Literal: take words at face value	◆ Literal: give examples	◆ Figurative: infer conclusions	◆ Symbolic: infer meaning and draw connections
Word clues/ words favourite	◆ Fun ◆ Boring ◆ Excitement ◆ 'Depends on the situation' ◆ Luck ◆ Now ◆ Action	◆ Experience (theirs and yours) ◆ In the past ◆ Who is responsible? ◆ Processes and procedures ◆ Better than, worse than ◆ First, second third, etc	◆ Strategy ◆ Will correct word choice in others ◆ Qualified statements 'If a and b, therefore c' ◆ Thus, and therefore, to draw logical conclusion from points ◆ 'As a result'	◆ Always ◆ Never ◆ Everyone ◆ Forever ◆ Huge ◆ Purpose ◆ Meaning ◆ Significance ◆ Connection

> Mindmate correcting the word choice of a soulmate describing
> the location for the wedding reception as a '*huge* tennnis court':
> 'As compared to a small tennis court?!'

Try it now

Words we use

Step 1:   Write down the words or subjects that you think are
          taboo in your relationship, those subjects that cause an
          emotional reaction in you.

Step 2:   Ask your partner to do the same thing.

Step 3:   Discuss your lists. What are the similarities? What are the
          differences?

What did you learn about your partner's hot buttons? What did
your partner learn about yours? What will you do with this data?

The way we say the words

The words we use provide the content, but the delivery and body
language provide the meaning. Have you ever been in a situation
when you are sharing a really important event with your partner
and they say 'I understand' in a disinterested voice while gazing at
the television: right words, wrong delivery! Compare it with
saying 'I understand' using a reassuring voice while making eye
contact and nodding. A totally different meaning is created.

> 'I call my partner "Computer Charlie" when he gets into his
> computer games and gives me this random "I understand!"'

Most communication goes astray, not because of the word
choice but because the delivery and body language is at odds with
the words we are using. Given a choice between believing the
words or the delivery/body language, we will always believe the
latter.

The greatest factor that can affect delivery is when we are
experiencing some type of emotion. This reaction can then cause
us to sound argumentative, hostile, disinterested, etc. Recognising
this emotional response can help us to better manage our tone,

inflection, volume, pitch, etc to ensure that the meaning is in alignment with the word choice. In the chapter on conflict we will describe in more detail assertive, submissive and aggressive communication.

In addition, each lovemate tends to deliver the message differently as shown in the following table.

Communication component	Playmate	Helpmate	Mindmate	Soulmate
Delivery	◆ Fast-paced and up-beat	◆ Deliberate and methodical	◆ Confident possibly to the point of arrogance	◆ Flowing and dramatic
Sequencing	◆ Tactical sequencing: either straight to the point or stories around a theme to make maximum impact	◆ Numerical sequencing: 1, 1a, 1b, 1c, 2, 2a, 2b, 2c, etc, preferring to begin at 1	◆ Starting with the big picture and sequencing by category	◆ Interconnected ideas around a theme although they may seem to be unconnected

Body language

> 'Sometimes we have difficulty communicating when we are having trouble reading the other's non-verbals or not really understanding first where the other person is coming from.'

Body language is also very important in providing the meaning of the message. It is an idiom we all speak, but few actually understand. It's an extremely complex form of expression. Below are a few factors to consider when communicating with your partner:

◆ One of the challenges in using body language when communicating with our mate is that many of the signals that we give are subconscious. We don't necessarily understand the messages we are sending. How many times has your partner said to you after an interaction 'You obviously were not listening!' The lack of concentrated eye contact, fidgeting, a body posture that is leaning away, nodding at the wrong time were all dead give-aways in terms of what we were really thinking! Our body language will always communicate our true feelings, despite what we say.

♦ In addition, our body language can also communicate attitude. How you feel on a certain day will show in your body language and in your voice. It's how you show interest. If you are annoyed with your partner, your body language will show it by such changes as tightening of facial expression, flashing eyes and turning away.

♦ When we are getting on well with our partner, we subconsciously pace or mirror their body language. We speak at the same speed, lean towards them, nod as they nod, etc. (See dating chapter.) Conversely, when we are upset with our partner we may subconsciously 'dispace' them. We may talk more slowly when they are talking quickly, we may move back or turn away. This dispacing can negatively affect the interaction. If we can learn to pace our partner in stressful interactions, we will increase the likelihood of a successful outcome.

♦ One of the most important things to remember when reading body language is that it is composed of a series of signals, not just one or two. Each partner will have his/her own unique series of body language cues. If you can learn to tune into these cues, and recognise their meaning, you will be able to avoid potential communication pitfalls. For instance, if your partner usually reflects before providing a response, without understanding their style you misread this response as lack of interest.

Each temperament also uses different body language cues, as shown in the following table.

Communication component	Playmate	Helpmate	Mindmate	Soulmate
Gestures	◆ Clawing with hands	◆ Finger-pointing and chopping with hand	◆ Pull ideas from the air ◆ Holding an inverted globe in one hand	◆ Circular hand gestures ◆ Both hands up and open
Body language	◆ May appear casual and laid back depending on company	◆ May appear deliberate and formal	◆ May appear distant and preoccupied	◆ May appear warm and open
Most obvious cue	◆ Fidgeting when bored or with inadequate sensory stimulation	◆ Respectful and contained	◆ Critical questioning and correction of words	◆ Empathetic and gracious
Skill in recognizing body language cues	◆ Very in tune with body language and physical cues	◆ If a nurturing helpmate will have empathy for other's body language ◆ If a regulating helpmate may miss visual cues	◆ May be oblivious to people's reactions as they drive to achieve their goal	◆ Pick up the emotional and interpersonal cues: will quote the impressions body language creates versus concrete data

Try it now

Observing body language and delivery

- ◆ To recognize your different styles of communicating, for one day each of you can observe your partner's body language.
- ◆ Watch his/her delivery and body language in terms of tone, pace, intonation, eye contact, gestures, movement, facial expression when he/she is stressed, excited, concerned, etc.
- ◆ Now discuss your observations with your partner. What did you see? What did you learn? How could this knowledge help you improve communication effectiveness?

Obtaining a response

> 'Dialogue – a way of having a conversation of equals that allows you to have and maintain your own point of view – while being able to understand another's.'
>
> *David Bohm*

The other critical part in the communication process is listening to our partner and encouraging them to communicate with us. Asking questions, listening and paraphrasing are critical skills in building two-way communication. We will be discussing these skills in more detail in the chapter on managing conflict.

Open-ended questions

There are two types of questions: **open-ended** and **closed**. Open-ended questions cannot be answered by a yes or no, and serve to open up communication between you and your partner. Open-ended questions begin with the words tell me about, describe, explain, who, what, where, when, why and how. Examples of open-ended questions are:

- What are some activities that you would enjoy?
- Why is this particular issue causing you more challenges than other issues?
- Describe the rationale for your approach.
- What is your goal?

> 'Why? Always, all ways a good question.'
>
> *Malcolm S. Forbes*

Make sure you allow time for a response: the time taken may be influenced by your partner's degree of introversion or extroversion. We will discuss this later in the chapter.

Closed questions

Closed questions can be answered by a yes or no and serve to gather specific data. They are used to close down a part of the conversation and to verify data. Often we use closed questions with our partner because of time limitations – or maybe we are not interested in the answer!

Examples of closed questions are:

* Do you agree?
* Is that all?
* Will you do this?

> 'It's better to ask some of the questions than to know all the answers.'
>
> *James Thurber*

Active listening

Good **listening** is one of the most complex communication skills. Yet at school we have normally spent over ten years being taught how to speak, while little instruction is given on how to listen. In our society power is viewed as going to the speaker rather than the listener, so we tend to view listening as a passive activity.

> 'Listening is a primitive art of love in which a person gives himself to another's word, making him accessible and vulnerable to that word.'
>
> *William Stringfellow*

In reality, listening is an active skill that provides control of the conversation to the individual who is listening: by really understanding the other person's viewpoint, we are better able to communicate our needs and wants from their perspective. Good listening is a prerequisite for an effective relationship. Below are a few ideas to help you and your partner improve your listening skills.

* Pay attention to your partner. Stop your mind from wandering as they are speaking.
* Process the information as they are speaking. Try to view the data from their perspective.
* Be patient if their communication style or pacing is different from yours.
* Paraphrase what the other person has said by restating their ideas in your own words.
* If you find yourself rehearsing ask questions to gather more data.

Gender influences

> 'He is not that interested in hearing many of the details of my day-to-day life: he's not a real "chit-chat" type of guy.'
>
> Female discussing communication with her mate

As we discussed in the valuing differences chapter, male and female differences plus gender differences can also affect the degree to which we use these skills. Often men will want to jump into solving the problem, whereas women are more comfortable communicating empathy as needed.

Try it now

Discussing an interest

This exercise will be conducted between you and your partner. The purpose is to practise asking open-ended questions, listening actively and paraphrasing.

Step 1:   You or your partner choose to be the interviewer, the other person will then be the interviewee.

Step 2:   The partner who is to be interviewed selects a topic from those listed below and tells the name of the subject to their interviewer.
    ◆ hobby
    ◆ vacation
    ◆ major accomplishment
    ◆ favourite job.

Step 3:   The person who is interviewing has *two to three minutes* to ask open-ended questions (at least five to ten) and listen actively to gather information on the topic selected.

Attention: The person who is being interviewed needs to provide the shortest possible answers to ensure their partner has to work hard at questioning. In addition, the person being interviewed should answer *no* if they hear a closed question.

Step 4:   At the end of the time, the person who has been interviewing paraphrases everything they have learned in the 30 seconds back to their partner.

Step 5:   The interviewee then gives feedback on how well the interviewer asked open-ended questions, listened actively, paraphrased and probed for specifics.

This exercise encourages both partners to practise open-ended questions, listening, paraphrasing and empathy – all critical skills in the communication process.

Adapting your style

The influence of introverting and extroverting

As we discussed in the chapter on loving style, the direction of our energy can either be external – it goes to the outer world of people and things first, known as extroverting – or to the inner world of ideas and reflection, known as introverting. We all live in both worlds, however we have a preference for one, and this preference can influence the communication process.

In the table below are a few tips to guide you and your partner so that you can become more in synch with each other, and gain a greater respect for the other perspective.

IF YOU OR YOUR PARTNER IS MORE EXTROVERTED	
He/she/you may:	To facilitate communication:
◆ Talk at length without apparent point – perceived as verbally excessive	◆ Try to think about the core of the idea first to make it more succinct
◆ Use more expressive body language	◆ Try to ensure that your gestures do not detract from the message
◆ Immediately jump in with an answer if a questions is asked	◆ Try to pause and look at other people's body language before answering
◆ Be uncomfortable with silence: saying something is better than nothing	◆ Try internally counting to ten before answering and listening to the silence
◆ Prefer to use the telephone or talk person-to-person	◆ Try to group ideas and select the right tool for the message
◆ Want a wide circle of friends	◆ Make sure the interaction is not so excessive there is never any 'alone time'

IF YOU OR YOUR PARTNER IS MORE INTROVERTED	
He/she/you may:	To facilitate communication:
◆ Not share all of their thoughts immediately	◆ Try to ask for more time to process when you need it
◆ Use more reserved body language	◆ Be prepared to give verbal cues about your thoughts after adequate time to process
◆ If a question is asked, may need time to pause before answering	◆ Try to, if possible, schedule a time for discussion so that you have time to reflect on the subject matter before the discussion
◆ Be comfortable with silence: saying nothing is better than 'verbal diarrhoea'	◆ Practise verbalizing externally what is going on at the time internally
◆ Prefer to use e-mail	◆ Try to select the right tool for the message
◆ Be reluctant to participate in parties or large social gatherings	◆ Find a balance. If it is important to your partner participate in exchange for one-to-one time later

The influence of temperament

Miscommunications can also occur because we are viewing the world through our own lens of temperament. It often behoves us to adapt our style when communicating with our partner, to try to smooth the interaction. Often in relationships we focus on changing the other person when in reality we know that the only person's behaviour we can directly influence is our own!

Adapting our style is not like stretching a rubber band – you try

> 'There's only one corner of the universe you can be certain of improving and that's your own self.'
>
> *Aldous Huxley*

briefly and then bounce back to your normal behaviour. Instead, it is more like stretching or working out a muscle: the more you flex it, the stronger it becomes. In addition, during the process of adapting to our partner's style, we develop a greater understanding and appreciation for their strengths and the quality of the relationship increases.

In order to adapt, you need to be able to step outside yourself and see your and your partner's behaviour, which is not an easy process. We are so much who we are, we often don't see it! Listed below are some ideas for smoothing communication with each lovemate.

Communicating with playmates

- Use short and more direct communication.
- Talk about concrete realities.
- Get to the point quickly and keep moving.
- Give feedback on their tactical competence.
- Expect cynicism and stories.
- Adapt to their colloquial language.
- Use tools and hands-on experiences when explaining approaches.
- Talk about impact, end results and variety.
- Remember that they read body language very accurately, so watch your body language cues.

Communicating with helpmates

- Talk about what was done in the past.
- Explain using a concrete, practical approach.
- Be specific about who is responsible for what in terms of roles and responsibilities.
- Explain steps sequentially, starting at the beginning and using numbering 1,2,3,4,5, etc.
- Be specific about the expected results.
- Expect questions about 'rules', 'what can and what cannot be done'.
- Use more conservative body language.
- Focus on efficiencies and process improvements.
- Provide lots of data and background information.

Communicating with mindmates

- Start with the big picture.

- Use precise language when explaining concepts and ideas.
- Give them an opportunity to analyse information and create new problem-solving approaches.
- Make sure of your facts and present relevant theoretical information where possible. Don't bluff!
- Don't take any critical questioning personally.
- Recognize their intellectual competence.
- Use analogies to make points.
- Attend to the conditional language, 'if this . . . then . . .'.
- Always explain what and why.
- Be prepared to debate possible approaches.

Communicating with soulmates

- Provide them with positive, genuine feedback.
- Be authentic when communicating – they will pick up fake conversation.
- Look for genuine points of connection.
- Focus on the purpose, big picture and conceptual ideas.
- Use metaphors and analogies.
- Talk about the benefits to people of actions: ability to develop potential and the greater good.
- Don't discount the global language and listen for the underlying meaning.
- Don't provide too much practical detail.
- Listen to their insights on people, which are usually accurate.

The influence of functions

Our functions also affect our communication, but not to the same extent. Our functions will produce some characteristic communication approaches that vary in the moment according to the function we are using. The chart following details some of these contributions.

As you can see, when you consider the personality differences against the backdrop of the complexity of the communication process, it is amazing we ever communicate effectively with our partner at all!

Function	Characteristics in Communication
Experiencing	◆ Talk about the experience and concrete details ◆ Tell stories ◆ Expressive and active body language
Recalling	◆ Talk about past sensory experiences in vivid detail ◆ Use a compare and contrast approach ◆ More reserved body language
Brainstorming	◆ Talk quickly about possibilities ◆ Verbal brainstorming ◆ Enthusiastic body language
Visioning	◆ More reserved body language, until the ideas comes to them: will want time to reflect on concepts ◆ The picture or idea will be described as a whole ◆ May justify with, 'I just know'
Systematizing	◆ Verbal pros and cons list ◆ Talk through the decision out loud ◆ Assertive and direct in tone and body language
Analyzing	◆ Will not communicate reasons or rationale unless challenged ◆ When external data does not match with internal criteria will argue a point ◆ Talk about models, theories and ideas
Harmonizing	◆ Show emotions on face and in body language ◆ Talk about personal details and self-disclose to connect ◆ Will talk about what's appropriate and not appropriate to them
Valuing	◆ Expressive about values when pushed or when beliefs are compromised ◆ Talk about 'what's right' or 'what's wrong' ◆ May appear easy-going or indifferent, until beliefs are challenged

Try it now

Adapting your style

Take it in turns to complete the following activity.

Step 1: Based on your partner's preference for introverting or extraverting, their temperament and their loving style, make a list of how you would adapt your style to improve the communication between you.

Step 2: Your partner then has the opportunity to provide you with feedback on the ideas you have listed. Remember not to get defensive: the purpose of this exercise is to strengthen that flexing muscle!

Providing positive feedback

> 'Under-appreciation is always the basis for our arguments.
> Always.'
>
> Mindmate discussing feedback

Feedback is any kind of attention you can get from or give to another person. It is essential for a positive partnership and is a fundamental human need. However, often in relationships we neglect to give our partner positive feedback as we are overwhelmed by day-to-day pressures, or competitiveness arises over who needs more attention. As a result our relationship is affected, and we run the risk that our partner will look elsewhere for positive input. However, by providing positive feedback we strengthen the relationship, build trust and increase mutual commitment.

The different types of feedback

There are several different types of input you can share with your partner: positive, developmental, negative and zero feedback.

Positive feedback will build your partner's self-esteem and provides a boost in spirit and enthusiasm. Examples are:

◆ praise
◆ thanks
◆ attention
◆ interest
◆ admiration.

> 'Kind words are short and easy to speak, but their echoes are truly endless.'
>
> *Mother Teresa*

Developmental feedback is given so that you can take a negative and turn it into a positive. Even though the intent with developmental feedback can be good, timing, delivery and the partner's desire to receive the feedback are important factors to consider.

Negative feedback is one of the worst types of feedback, because it is degrading and hurtful. It tends to happen when we are angry or we do not consider our words. We lash out with the result that everyone normally loses: you regret your outburst, and your partner may close down to you.

Zero feedback is simply the lack of any kind of feedback, positive or negative. it is even worse than negative feedback because it makes your partner feel unappreciated, unwanted and unneeded.

Unfortunately, in relationships we tend to rely on the last three and forget the first. In fact, when we conducted the research for this book and we asked couples how they provided feedback to each other, 90 per cent of the comments they made were about providing negative or developmental feedback.

In addition there is **conditional** and **unconditional feedback**.

Conditional feedback is expected and planned. It comes in response to special occasions. Examples are:

◆ Christmas cards
◆ birthday presents.

Unconditional feedback is much more fun and more appreciated. Examples are:

◆ an unexpected romantic date
◆ some unexpected positive feedback
◆ a surprise outing.

Many researchers have compared the effect of feedback with a bank's debit and credit balance. If you have a credit balance of feedback, you probably feel positive or energized. If you have a debit balance you are more likely to feel less motivated and depressed. A positive feedback balance for both partners provides a positive setting for the relationship.

General guidelines for giving positive feedback

> 'We talk and discuss a lot. We're very supportive and give praise easily.'
> Improvizing playmate discussing providing positive feedback to her actualizing soulmate

Yet providing positive feedback is not as easy as it seems. If the feedback is perceived as insincere or irrelevant we can actually lose 'brownie points'! Feedback should be precise in relating to the person receiving it.

In the table below are some guidelines for providing positive feedback, put into the acronym PRECISE.

P: Precise	Say specifically what you appreciate about your partner. There's nothing worse than 'you're great' – at what?!

R: Relevant	Make sure the feedback is related to something your partner values
	  – Playmates like frequent, to the point feedback on their talents and performance.
	  – Helpmates like feedback on concrete results and fulfilment of responsibilities, with recognition of their accomplishments.
	  – Mindmates like feedback on their competence and acknowledgement of their ideas, intellectual property and prowess.
	  – Soulmates like feedback on how they are unique and how they have made a difference, gently delivered.

E: Examples	Give examples to illustrate the point and make the feedback real.
C: Current	The more quickly you can give the feedback the better: for temperaments other than helpmates, memory of specific actions may fade quickly.
I: Interesting	Look at unconditional or unusual ways to provide positive feedback.
S: Sincere	Probably one of the most important factors: if you are not sincere, it will show. Your body language will give it away. So if you can't be sincere, wait until you can.
E: Elicit	Because we are so unaccustomed to receiving positive feedback, we may tend to brush it off: 'no, it's nothing', bounce it back: 'you are too' or block it with body language. It is our responsibility to ensure that our partner really hears what we have said by eliciting an acknowledging response from them.

Each lovemate also uses his/her own style to provide feedback:

Lovemate	Providing feedback
Playmate	◆ Can give surprise creative feedback and keep things light-hearted.

	◆ Provides timely feedback on current experience. ◆ May have to be careful with humour so as not to offend. ◆ May be too blunt.
Helpmate	◆ Will give lots of relevant examples in a structured way. ◆ Will probably focus on rating against others. ◆ May be too detailed with a focus on constructive feedback. ◆ May allow feelings to build up before providing feedback.
Mindmate	◆ Provides very precise feedback. ◆ Quick to give attention to competence: this is valuable feedback from a mindmate. ◆ May have to be moderate in pointing out negatives. ◆ May have to remind themselves to point out positives, even though they perceive this to be redundant.
Soulmate	◆ Able to recognise the uniqueness on which to provide positive feedback. ◆ Unconsciously provides genuine positive feedback. ◆ May not emphasise areas for improvement enough: don't like to broach negatives. ◆ May also have trouble being specific with impressions.

Try it now

Write a love letter to your partner noting all of the characteristics and traits you love about him/her.

Now discuss the letter with your partner. How did you feel?

Case Study

Henry and Marie focus on improving their communication

Henry is an introverted nurturing helpmate and Marie is an extroverting actualizing soulmate. Looking at their profile, it looks like this:

Personality Characteristic	Henry	Marie
Temperament	Helpmate	Soulmate
Information–gathering function	Recalling	Visioning
Decision-making function	Harmonising	Harmonising
Direction of energy	Introverting	Extroverting
Loving style	Introverted nurturer	Extroverted actualizer

Marie and Henry have been married for 25 years, and in that time have experienced many of the frustrations of caring deeply for a partner, but communicating on different plains. Marie was introduced to the concepts of type and temperament in her role as training consultant. She immediately saw the applicability for these ideas to communication with her partner: as a soulmate, one of her main interests was attending self-development workshops with Henry. Initially Henry was not particularly interested in the subject, it appeared too abstract (he prefers more concrete subjects) and he had no experience with the subject (recalling). Until he could see a practical application (helpmate), he expressed superficial interest, which of course was immediately apparent to Marie (harmonizing and soulmate's empathy). The practical application became obvious when Marie and Henry had a disagreement about their business. Marie had presented a large proposal to a high-tech company, and felt that the meeting had not gone well. As a result, she believed that she would not get the work that was important to the business. Henry's comment was 'Why would you think you could get that business anyway?' On the surface that could have been perceived to be a non-supportive comment. On closer analysis, and with an understanding of their differing communication styles, Marie was able to understand Henry's viewpoint and also explain to him the different functions each of them was using. She was very future focused (soulmate) with a picture of the business that she found hard to articulate (visioning). Henry relied on historical data (recalling) and was working from the data that Marie had never won a piece of business that size before. His comment was not a criticism, rather an observation. She was able to adapt to his style by citing examples of other consultants who had completed large projects of that size for the same company (providing experience for his recalling). He, in turn, gained a greater understanding of why she seemed so 'out there' sometimes, as he understood the future picture her visioning created.

Over time they each gained respect of the other person's viewpoint. As Marie built a successful business, Henry realised that her soulmate interest in people was also supported by the drive to make her vision a reality. This resulted in economic benefits for both of them. More and more, when she would indicate ideas from visioning, Henry would support her in their implementation: 'I don't know how you know, but I believe you.' In the same way Marie learned from Henry's helpmate questions 'What difference will this make at 9am on a Monday?' She focused on making her training programmes more concrete and tangible, and would consistently ask Henry for his input on exercises. When she wanted to play in the abstract world, she had other consultants who worked with her in the business who could do that. When Henry wanted to play in the concrete world, Marie had a greater understanding for his need to tinker with cars and fix things around the house. In addition, the fact that both Henry and Marie shared harmonising meant that they wanted a productive interaction and conflict related to style differences was very hurtful to them.

Early in their relationship, Marie's preference for extraverting also placed strain on their interaction: her need to socialise was at odds with Henry's need for quiet time for reflection. As they matured Marie learned to be comfortable with quiet time, and Henry found that with fewer social events he was better able to enjoy the activities.

Both Marie and Henry consciously focused on obtaining feedback from their partner, actually both using harmonising made this process a lot easier. In addition, they made an effort not only to give positive feedback, but also to accept it when they received it. Henry, as with many helpmates, tended to be modest about his own strengths and would seek developmental rather than positive feedback. Marie, as with many soulmates, had a high need for positive feedback, and Henry learned how to provide feedback that was more relevant to her, based around her making a difference versus fulfilling a responsibility.

As you can see, rather than becoming frustrated by their partner, they were able to adapt their style, which resulted in a closer relationship, and a greater sense of satisfaction with the partnership. They realised that, after all, they do have the same amount in common as when they were first introduced!

Discussion points

1. When you completed the exercise on words you use, what differences did you see in the taboo words you used versus your partner? What were your partner's hot buttons? What did you learn about yours? How could you use this information to improve communication with your partner? How could you manage any misunderstandings that arise from these different choices of words?

2. When you described an interesting event how was your delivery and body language similar to your partner? Different from your partner? How do these differences help the relationship? When do they hinder the effectiveness of the interaction?

3. When you conducted the exercise practising asking open-ended questions, listening and paraphrasing, how easy was it for you to ask open-ended questions? To what extent did you ask closed questions? How easy was it to listen and not talk?

How could you use these techniques to greater benefit in your relationship?

4. When you try to adapt your style, how easy is it? How are the differences between introverting and extroverting affecting your relationship? To what extent do you stay in your own style? To what extent do you adapt to your partner's? How could you become more aware of your own style?

5. When you reviewed positive feedback, to what extent do you provide positive feedback to your partner? How often do they provide feedback to you? Did you complete the love letter to your partner? What did you learn from that exercise? How could you incorporate positive feedback into your daily routine?

Summary

In this chapter you have been given a comprehensive overview of the communication process and the skills needed to communicate with your partner. In addition, we looked at how our temperament can cause us to speak a different language. By adapting our style, we can reduce some of the misinterpretations that occur when communicating with someone who is different from us and learn to truly appreciate our partner's perspective.

We learned the following information about communication skills:

♦ The communication process is extremely complex.

♦ Sending the message effectively to our partner involves choosing the right words, using delivery to enhance the message, and being aware at all times of body language and using it as a tool to improve rather than detract from the message.

♦ Equally important to sending the message is to ensure we receive feedback from our partner throughout any interaction. This involves using open-ended questions, listening and paraphrasing.

♦ When we communicate with our partner we need to understand their direction of energy (introverting and extroverting), their temperament (playmate, helpmate, etc) and function they are using at the time. Once we do, we can consciously adapt our style to not only improve communication, but build commonality with our partner.

◆ Finally, in order to build a sustainable relationship, couples need to ensure that they remember to provide each other with positive feedback on a regular basis, which provides reassurance and motivation for both partners.

CHAPTER 7

*The harder
the conflict,
the more
glorious the
triumph*

Relating: Dealing with Conflicts

C onflict arises in every relationship, no matter how strong the partnership appears. Managed effectively, conflict can be a positive factor in identifying and overcoming differences, and deepening the level of communication between the couple.

However, people vary in their approach to, and feelings about, conflict. By learning about our own and our partner's approach to disagreements, and applying techniques to control these situations, we can successfully resolve issues before they erode the quality of the relationship.

Defining conflict

Conflict can be defined both literally and figuratively as any disagreement or struggle with another person. In relationships, it is helpful to remember:

◆ Conflict is natural and inevitable because people view the world differently.

◆ Conflict, if harnessed properly, can be a motivator for change.

◆ Conflict can be constructive or destructive; it really depends on the way it is handled.

◆ Conflict can result in learning, growth and co-operation for the partnership.

◆ Conflict can be managed to minimise losses and maximise gains for all involved.

◆ Conflict is frequently accompanied by tension.

Recognizing sources of conflict

There are many different sources of conflict in relationships centred on the mesh of temperaments, values, family, interaction between the partners, and the context in which the couple is based. Some of these sources were discussed in earlier chapters, let's look at some examples of each.

Relationship-related conflicts

> 'Our biggest sources of conflict are in terms of us competing with each other, in terms of time and valuing the other person's contribution.'
>
> Mindmate on his conflicts with his partner

- differences in values
- different personalities
- different cultures
- jealousy
- competition
- 'she reminds me of my mother'
- unexpressed needs
- different perceptions
- assumptions
- prejudices
- resentments
- under-appreciation
- unknown expectations.

Contextual

> 'We also sometimes have conflicts over finances because I am more frugal than he is.'
>
> Soulmate on conflicts with her playmate partner

- not performing agreed tasks
- managing finances
- sharing of workload
- disciplining children
- family responsibilities
- vacation/holiday needs.

Many conflicts are usually a muddy combination of a variety of factors.

Try it now

Sources of conflict in your relationship
Write down what your partner does that angers you.

Talk it through:

- Which are related to the external environment?
- Which of these items are characteristics and which are behaviours?
- Is there a flip side to any of the qualities that you appreciate?

Understanding your response to conflict

Before we introduce skills and techniques to help manage conflict situations, let's look at how you and your partner respond in a conflict situation.

> 'We get defensive, attack each other and then I usually cry.'
> Helpmate on her and her partner's response to conflict

Try it now

How do you respond in a conflict situation?

Think of a time when you had a conflict with your partner.

1. What was the conflict situation?
2. What was your emotional response? How did you feel?
3. What was your immediate reaction? What did you do?
4. What was the result?

Communicating assertively

As you can see from the above exercise, many of us react emotionally in a conflict situation. This emotion causes us to activate our fight or flight response, which results in either an aggressive (fight) or a submissive (flight) style of communication. Both these styles result in a win-lose experience and escalation of the conflict.

> 'People who fight fire with fire usually end up with ashes.'
> *Abigail van Buren*

Instead we need to use **assertive communication** to facilitate a discussion and a win-win outcome. Let's look at each of these communication styles in more detail.

Aggressive communication

Aggressive communication is defined as standing up for our own rights in such a way that the other person's rights are violated. It's when we express thoughts, feelings and beliefs in unsuitable and inappropriate ways, even if we honestly view our beliefs to be right.

> 'If we get into an argument, he will start speaking in a loud voice and can sometimes be very harsh whereas I tend to get very quiet and take things personally.'
> Soulmate describing her partner's aggressive behaviour and her submissive response

Aggression gives us the advantage at the expense of our relationship and often serves to degrade our partner's needs. It leads to a closedown in communication and an escalation of a conflict situation. For instance, if asked by our significant other for something that's completely unrealistic (a fairly common occurrence!), such as 'I want you to clear out the garage today because we are having friends over for dinner' the reply could be:

◆ Aggressive: You have got to be kidding – that's ridiculous! Who is going to look in the garage anyway?

Submissive communication

Submissive communication is defined as failing to stand up for our rights or we express them in a way that allows our partner to easily disregard them. We are submissive when we express our thoughts, values and beliefs in an apologetic, cautious, self-effacing manner or when we fail to express our ideas at all. We also might use long, justifying explanations, putting ourselves down while submitting to the wants and needs of the other person.

> 'He ploughs through it and I stick my head in the sand.'
> Soulmate describing her partner's aggressive behaviour and her submissive response

This can lead to a win-lose experience, where neither party is satisfied.

◆ As above, when faced with the same request, the submissive reply could be: I guess I could do that . . . it will take me all day, but I suppose I could . . .

Assertive communication

Both aggressive and submissive communication are automatic and somewhat unconscious as they originate from the body's fight or flight response. **Assertive communication** is the most misunderstood. It is defined as standing up for our own rights, in a way that does not violate our partner's. It requires a conscious and deliberate choice as it supersedes our body's natural reactions, leading to the open and honest communication of our own point of view, while showing we understand our partner's position. For instance, with that same request the reply could be:

◆ Assertive: I understand you want our home to appear tidy for our guests. However, they probably will not come out into the garage. Let's focus our energies on the areas they will see.

> 'The relationship comes first: if there's conflict we always look at how to resolve it so that we'll end up better, not worse.'
> Playmate describing assertive communication with her
> mindmate partner

Try it now

Assertive communication

Step 1: Make a wish list of things you want from your partner.

Step 2: Pick one thing that is really important to you.

Step 3: Ask for what you want from your partner using the following principles:

  – know exactly what you want
  – be specific
  – time your request appropriately
  – be brief
  – ask in an open-ended, non-demanding way
  – make sure that an edge does not come into your voice
  – try another method if the first doesn't work.

Managing conflict situations

> 'Don't let anger fester too long. Make the first move towards reconciliation.'
>
> *James Dobson*

When faced with a conflict in the relationship there is a tendency to try to jump to a solution, before gathering enough data on the real causes of the conflict. In this section we introduce you to a process to help you PAUSE before deciding how to resolve the conflict. Understanding and practising the skills in the PAUSE technique will help you to work through even the most challenging situations.

The steps in the PAUSE technique are:

P: Recognise that there is a Problem
A: Address emotions: both yours and your partner's
U: Understand each other's positions
S: Find Shared interests
E: Explore options.

P: recognise the problem

Earlier in this chapter we talked about some of the potential sources of conflict between you and your partner. Normally there will be signals that a problem is present, which might include:

- a feeling of resentment
- cross words without obvious cause
- partner becoming more quiet
- increase in anxiety.

A: address emotions: yours and your partner's

The first factor you have to address when trying to resolve conflict is to somehow manage your emotional response. We can feel defensive, aggressive, impatient, annoyed or upset, to name just a few emotions.

As you can see from the graph in Figure 12, the more emotional you are the lower your level of logic is. Even if a resolution is the ideal, you and your partner will not hear it because one of you is still upset. Conversely, when emotions are low the logic is high

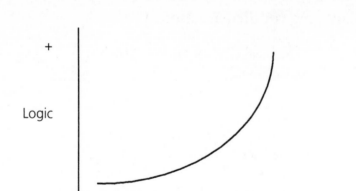

Fig. 12. Reasoning an emotions graph.

and we are more likely to be able to move on to resolution.

'Usually he will either give in or I'll give up. Reactions: I get upset and he withdraws or gets mad.'

On responding to each other's hot buttons

In relationships we tend to press our partner's hot buttons. Some ideas that have helped reduce the emotional response to hot buttons are:

♦ Take a deep breath (being careful not to exhale with a big sigh!). This will control your breathing and help to manage your body's stress response.

♦ Mentally step back and look at the big picture: ask yourself what it really means at the end of the day.

♦ Think about the seriousness of the problem. Often problems are not as severe as they appear when we are upset.

♦ Sometimes it can be a good thing to take a break and regroup for the discussion when emotions have cooled a little, providing you do revisit the problem.

♦ Realise that your partner is probably not deliberately attacking you. He/she is probably angry because of the situation or because of other pressures in his/her life and you just happen to be on the receiving end.

Try it now

Calming emotions
1. How can you calm your emotions?
2. How will your partner calm their emotions?
3. What commitments will you make in the future to dealing with your emotions in a conflict situation?

U: understand each other's positions

The third step in the PAUSE technique involves understanding each other's positions. Positions may be based around money, task allocation, conditions or outcomes. This focus often produces a better than/worse than comparison where partners compare, contrast and compete about the issues, rather than try to understand them, which usually results in a negative outcome.

However, behind each partner's position there are normally shared and aligned interests. By identifying and understanding each other's positions you will be able to comprehend the underlying shared interests which are at the root of resolving the conflict.

Two essential skills are used to understand the other person's position, discussed initially in the communicating chapter. In conflict situations we use a more specific version of each:

◆ listening: **generous listening**
◆ paraphrasing: **empathy statements**.

Generous listening

'Generous listening involves listening with a deep appreciation for the feelings, reality and commitment of your partner. It contributes to both partners' experience of being understood.'

Julie Khademi

◆ Generous listening is not automatic listening, which involves selective filters, assumptions, or expectations that shape our understanding of the message in a way that limits or distorts its intended meaning.
◆ Generous listening is imperative when there is a conflict between you and your mate. It means you listen with your ears,

your eyes and your heart. You listen for content, for feeling and for meaning. You listen for behaviour, using your right and left brain, your intuition and your senses. You listen for congruence between what you hear, what you see and what you sense.

◆ You listen for:

  −   the content or the reason why they are feeling upset or frustrated

  −   the feeling or emotion they are expressing.

> 'It's great to be great, but it's greater to be human.'
>
> *Will Rogers*

Try it now

Generous listening exercise

For the following statement identify both the content (the reason the person is feeling dissatisfied) and the feelings (the range of emotions) being expressed. The answers are at the end of the section.

Situation

This is the third time you promised you would do the shopping, and there's no food in the house again.

1. Identify the content (reason the person is dissatisfied).
2. Identify the feelings (emotions being expressed).

Answers

This is the third time you have promised you would do the shopping, and there's no food in the house again.

Content: no food in the house/broken promise.

Feelings: partner feels let down as a commitment has been broken, tired and hungry.

Normally the content, or the reason the person is upset, is fairly easy to fix. However, if the problem is fixed without the person feeling heard the resolution will not be viewed as acceptable. You may have fixed the problem, but you have not fixed the relationship issues. At the end of this section you will have an opportunity to try each of these skills with one of your current conflicts.

Empathy statements

In generous listening we identified the content or reason the person was dissatisfied and the feelings being expressed. Now we have to empathise with our partner to show we understand both the reason they are upset, and the feelings they are experiencing. Because of upbringing and society men often have more trouble with empathising with feelings, as they try to push for resolution.

> 'Empathy is defined as the ability to put yourself in the other person's shoes to understand their frame of reference.'

♦ Demonstrating the feeling of empathy for our partner is important. If we are face-to-face, empathy is easier to show. Using body language such as nodding, having a sympathetic expression, leaning towards our partner, etc can all indicate concern.

♦ One of the greatest challenges with empathy statements is making them sound *genuine*. We have to develop our own style of communicating in tense situations, showing we understand our partner's viewpoint without sounding trite or glib. Practice makes perfect.

> 'We try to openly discuss our differences and come to some compromises.'
>
> Helpmate approaching conflict

♦ In relationships it can often be difficult to empathise with our partner's perspective because we are holding on to our own position. However, when you use empathy statements you are verbally crossing to your partner's 'side' in order to demonstrate you understand their predicament. Your partner then often follows you back to 'your side' to resolve the issues. Empathy statements allow both sides to move *from their positions to areas of common interest*.

The way we express empathy verbally is to:

♦ **Rephrase the content,** restating the reason the other person is upset in your own words.

♦ **Reflect the feeling** putting the emotions you are interpreting from the other person into words.

Examples of empathising with a partner on having a heavy workload:

♦ I can understand *you are feeling tired* (feeling) because *your project at work has taken much longer than you thought it would* (content).

♦ It *can be frustrating* (feeling) when *the people you are relying on let you down* (content).

♦ If I was *carrying your workload* (content), *I'd be feeling overwhelmed* (feeling) too.

'I wish he were more compassionate towards me. I feel like I would have to drop dead before he realised that I am burned out.'

Helpmate about her mindmate partner

'She is much more needy in terms of getting support.'

The other side

Don't just say: 'I understand'. Such a statement is a cliché. You may hear your partner say in reply 'you don't understand – you're not standing here hungry at 7:30 at night with no food in the house.' If you use 'I understand', make sure you include *what you understand* (the reason your partner is upset) and *the feeling you are hearing* (the emotions they are expressing).

Try it now

Creating empathy statements

Write an empathizing statement for the scenario about shopping we introduced on page 156, restating the content (the reason they are upset) and reflecting the feelings (the emotions they are expressing).

Answers

Three possible ideas are:

♦ I can understand you're feeling *let down* (reflect the feeling) because I have not done the shopping as we agreed (restate the content).

♦ You must be feeling *hungry and tired* (reflect the feeling) *with no food in the house* (restate the content).

- I know it is *frustrating* (reflect the feeling) when we agree something and *then my schedule prevents me from fulfilling my side of the bargain* (restate the content).

S: find shared interests

> Moving away from positions to exploring interests allows for problem-solving together. By identifying interests, you move one step closer to resolving the conflict.

Interests represent needs, desires, concerns and fears. They are often silent within or behind the conflict. Some interests are the same and some will differ. Those that differ will often get all the attention in a conflict. When you can focus on shared interests first, you may be able to resolve the issue before you have to deal with differing positions. Many of the couples we worked with shared the following interests:

- Building a productive relationship.
- Coming to an agreement with the minimum of pain.
- Deep caring for each other.
- Shared values and beliefs.
- Commitment to the partnership.

> 'I don't feel like the bottom is going to fall out whenever we have an argument because the foundation of our bond is always there.'
>
> On shared interests

E: explore options

The best way to explore **options** is to brainstorm different possibilities, with no restrictions. Guidelines for brainstorming options are:

- No judgement on ideas.
- More is better.
- Everything is written down.
- Both partners participate.
- Think about lessons learned.
- It's okay to piggyback on ideas.
- No voting while brainstorming.

Try it now

> **Using the PAUSE technique to resolve a conflict**
> **P**roblem
> Step 1:   List some of the issues that are causing conflict between you and your partner. What are the signals that these issues are present? Are they temporary or long-term?
>
> **A**ddress emotions
> Step 2:   Identify, for these issues, how you and your partner will manage your emotions so that you can begin the conflict resolution process. How will you ensure that you don't press each other's hot buttons?
>
> **U**nderstand each other's positions
> Step 3:   State your position and your partner's position.
> Step 4:   Write an empathy statement for your partner's position that you will use. Make sure your partner writes an empathy statement for your position.
>
> Find **S**hared interests
> Step 5:   What are the interests you share in this situation?
>
> **E**xplore options
> Step 6:   What are some options you can use to meet these shared interests? If the problems are temporary, how could you both alleviate them? If the problems are long-term, what have you been doing to address them?

Making decisions

When you have generated options for resolving the conflict, you are ready to make a decision on what actions will work best. If you try to make a decision without using the PAUSE technique, the decision will be viewed as a win/lose because both parties may still be irate or locked into their positions.

> 'Unfortunately Chris tried a conflict resolution option without going through the steps in the PAUSE technique first. He brought home a videotape on making relationships work, and started playing it. I still felt misunderstood at this point; I was still upset and fixed in my position. As a result, I showed no interest and Chris became even more frustrated. So he raised the volume to blaring loud. The conflict escalated instead of the other way around!'

By using the PAUSE technique both partners will be positioned to make a reasonable decision.

There are several different types of decision-making approaches, which revolve around the concepts of win/win or win/lose.

- The win/win decision is a new option or approach that both parties are happy with.
- The win/win compromise predicates that while this resolution might not be the absolutely ideal result for both partners, it is a decision that both can live with.
- A win/lose decision means that one person in the partnership wins and the other loses. While the ultimate goal is for both partners to be committed to every decision, it is also unrealistic to expect win/win agreements in every aspect of living and interacting together.

Win/win joint decision-making

> 'We look at how the decision affects the big picture. We look at the pros and cons of doing or not doing something. We don't do anything until we have come to an agreement. We try to get agreement about underlying principles so that we don't get hung up on differences over minor details.'
>
> On win/win joint decision-making

Joint decision-making is the most effective win/win approach and normally results in a high quality result. A decision is reached when both partners can agree the final outcome. It occurs only after there has been full participation in the conflict resolution process, with active discussion of the advantages and disadvantages of the issue and both partners' positions. Compromise is not the same as joint decision-making. When there is a compromise one person has given up on their perspective, and will often view the decision as a 'lose' for them. However, joint decision-making is usually more time consuming and can require high level skills. Joint decision-making appears best for major life decisions.

To facilitate joint decision-making you can:

- Combine and summarize similar ideas.

- Narrow down a long list by discussing top choices.
- Eliminate unlikely choices.
- Discuss pros and cons of top choices, using logic and facts to support ideas.
- Allow disagreements to be discussed until they are resolved.
- Summarize and review final lists.
- Make the decision.
- Ensure both partners agree with the decision.

Win/win individual decision-making

> 'Moving back to LA was bad for my career, but we both knew it was the best thing to do in the interests of our relationship. It was easy for me to do, but I think she bore some guilt about me making that decision.'
>
> On win/win individual decision-making

The other mode of making win/win decisions is to jointly decide who in the partnership can make that decision. For instance, a couple, when furnishing a house separated the joint and individual decisions in the following way.

Joint decisions were:
- selecting the furniture
- choosing pictures
- agreeing the colours.

Individual decisions were:
- selecting the contractor
- buying the TV and stereo.

This approach may be justified in terms of speed when decisions are not that important, or when it is agreed that one partner is better suited to make the decision on a particular area.

Try it now

Decision with your partner

Step 1: Make a list of some of the decisions you have made with your partner.

Step 2: Evaluate to what extent it was possible or necessary to achieve a joint solution.

Step 3: For these decisions, how many were achieved by joint and individual win/win approaches? How many were achieved by win/lose? Which partner won and which lost?

Step 4: How could you ensure more balanced decision-making in the future?

Loving styles and conflict

Lovemates

On top of the complexity of managing conflict with someone we care deeply about is the added complexity of how each lovemate approaches conflict differently.

> **Snapshot of temperaments in conflict**
> 'In any conflict I prefer to work through it, come to a decision and move on.'
>
> *Playmate*
>
> 'When we are both upset, we stop and wait. Then we discuss differences and come up with a solution.'
>
> *Helpmate*
>
> 'We constantly fight over whose life is more difficult.'
>
> *Mindmate*
>
> 'I think we were both destined to be together despite some very turbulent times.'
>
> *Soulmate*

The tables following summarise some of the inherent strengths and potential challenges that each temperament faces in approaching conflict.

Additionally, the degree to which a person wants to talk or think it through before talking will be influenced by their preference for introverting and extroverting. Those with an extroverting preference may 'vent' immediately. Those with an introverting preference may go inside and 'stew'.

Sensitivity to our partner's natural tendency will also help in resolving conflict.

> 'I like to resolve conflict quickly by bringing it to a head and getting it over with. She usually wants to let the feelings ride a bit more.'
>
> On the introverting/extroverting difference

Functions

Remember that the differing use of functions can affect the resolution of the conflict. In addition, although we tend to prefer to use two specific functions (as shown in the table in the appendix), we can have access to all eight. Learning to use different functions, depending on the stage of conflict resolution, can help reduce the escalation of conflict.

Lovemate	Strengths	Challenges
Playmate	◆ Quick to see current problems ◆ Quickly recognize the most expedient tactical solution and will want to implement it now! ◆ See creative contextual options for fixing the problems	◆ May forget to consider future implications of solutions ◆ May need help in slowing down to listen to their partner's perspective ◆ May get impatient with what appear as unnecessary discussions around interests and needs
Helpmate	Approach conflict resolution in a step-by-step, structured and methodical way ◆ Gravitate to solutions that respect the traditions of the relationship ◆ Will consider their partner in the resolution	◆ May have diffulculty seeing beyond the shoulds and ought tos ◆ May appear slow moving into problem-solving and decision-making as they consider options ◆ May appear too cautious and reluctant to take completely new approaches
Mindmate	◆ Use critical thinking to perceive problems quickly – naturally consider what's missing ◆ Approach conflict resolution from an abstract, conceptual perspective ◆ Pay less attention to past or current experience, but will look to pinpoint 'the' source of conflict	◆ May have difficulty understanding the practicality behind implementing a solution and appear to oversimplify issues ◆ May not consider the people issues sufficiently in the analysis of information ◆ May struggle with expressing genuine empathy for their partner's perspective
Soulmate	◆ Will recognize a source of conflict, even before there are obvious signs ◆ Understand and be able to empathize with their partner's position: will be able to build bridges between different viewpoints ◆ Identify many options and are future focused in considering options	◆ May miss consideration of practical options ◆ May want to 'over-solve' the conflict – go for a difficult and distant ideal ◆ May not pay enough attention to logical objective criteria and find it difficult to disconnect from their partner if they are both in pain

WHEN USING THE PAUSE TECHNIQUE		
	Approach	Possible challenges
Experiencing	◆ Able to recognize body language signals so will be aware of conflict ◆ Will be great at creating options to explore ◆ Flexible and quick thinking in approach	◆ May be reluctant to follow a structured process: want to bounce around ◆ May want to push for action versus following the PAUSE technique ◆ May get distracted by the current context
Recalling	◆ Will approach the PAUSE technique in a sequential, structured manner ◆ Will bring options that have worked in the past to the discussion ◆ More deliberate and thoughtful in approach and comfortable with pausing for reflection	◆ May need time to access their rich store of data ◆ May bring prior conflicts into the current conflict 'last time . . . happened' and be negative about solutions that have not been tried before ◆ May attempt a 'better than, worse than' rating in terms of positions rather than focusing on shared interests
Brainstorming	◆ Naturally able to brainstorm possible solutions to problems and new approaches to conflict ◆ Will focus on the patterns and meanings in the conflict beyond the obvious data to gain a more complete understanding ◆ Resourceful and upbeat – normally see the positive opportunities in the problems	◆ May not consider the practical implementation side of the options they suggest ◆ May want to make all changes at once and be reluctant to defer any ideas ◆ May see patterns and meanings that are not there
Visioning	◆ Reflect and then develop an entire solution to the conflict ◆ Picture entirely new ways of approaching the conflict ◆ Will be comfortable pausing before action, because this is the way they naturally function	◆ May be reluctant to accept anyone else's solution, in part or in whole ◆ May see the entire cause of the conflict as an entirety instead of as components ◆ May not be able to clearly articulate the change or solution

WHEN MAKING DECISIONS		
	Approach	Possible challenges
Systematizing	◆ Creating a pros and cons list to evaluate criteria including cause and effect assumptions, 'if this, then this . . .'	◆ May be frustrated when they cannot understand a resolution in terms of cause/effect ◆ May become frustrated by what they

	◆ Able to design the implementation of the resolution ◆ Anticipate the consequences of decisions and act to handle them	perceive to be an emotional response ◆ May find it hard to understand a course of action that is not logical
Analyzing	◆ Enjoy the objective process of analysing possible solutions and critically evaluating the options for their effectiveness ◆ Strategic – explore innovative ideas without the push for practical implementation (Mindmates only) ◆ Observe the process and reflect and analyze it throughout the conflict	◆ Own logic might not agree with their partner's resolution ◆ The course of action may not make sense with their internal decision ◆ May want to continuously change and analyze as issues arise
Harmonizing	◆ Will want to ensure that his/her partner supports the decision ◆ Understand what is important to their partner from a subjective perspective ◆ Sensitive to his/her partner's feelings	◆ May find it difficult to distance themselves and analyze cause and effect data ◆ May not add their own perspective in order to maintain harmony and consensus ◆ May have difficulty making decisions, if there is conflict
Valuing	◆ Value individual's different perspectives and allow them to express their opinions ◆ Consider 'is this right?' 'Is this the right direction to be going in?' ◆ Consider the ethics of the solution in relation to their own values	◆ May not work towards a joint decision if it goes against their beliefs ◆ May find it difficult to voice their reasons for specific decisions ◆ May withdraw emotionally when their beliefs system is offended

Case Study

In this case study we examine a conflict about finances for a new couple Jason and Julie. Jason is an introverting actualizer and Julie is an introverting improvizer.

Personality	Jason	Julie
Lovemate	Soulmate	Playmate
Information-gathering	Visioning	Experiencing
Decision-making	Harmonizing	Valuing
Direction of energy	Introverting	Introverting
Loving style	Introverted actualizer	Introverted improvizer

Jason and Julie have been married for 18 months. Jason works for a retail company where he is the Vice President of Inventory Planning and Julie runs her own business doing visual design work. Jason is seven years older than Julie and is an actualizing soulmate using harmonizing and visioning. Julie is an improvizing playmate.

Julie says, 'We have a very wonderful relationship. We're best friends and have a lot of fun. We support each other in many ways, which is especially helpful when the fun part wears off. We share a lot of the same interests: cooking, exercise, reading, entertaining, dancing, travelling and going to a lot of concerts.'

Areas for conflict

There have been two areas of conflict for Julie and Jason as they build their relationship: finances and peer counselling. Jason conducts co-counselling sessions with groups in the evening and it was very important for him that Julie share that interest. Unfortunately, Julie had been brought up in a family that was intensely private. In addition her strongest function was valuing which in itself is a more personal decision-making function compared with Jason's use of harmonizing. Initially Jason was really disappointed that Julie found this process difficult, and it caused him to doubt the relationship as soulmates have a tendency to do if their mate is not perfect! In time, and with commitment, Julie has become more comfortable, and Jason has been able to empathize with her as she builds her competence and comfort level in this interest.

Recognize there is a problem

The finances have proved to present a more long-term conflict as with many couples. Jason and Julie approached them very differently. Jason was very organized, methodical and prudent. Julie tended to be more spontaneous and she says 'quite honestly, finances bore me to tears.' The problem surfaced because they started to have arguments over the finances: Jason earned approximately three times as much as Julie, however Julie tended to fritter away what she had. When Jason would question her on that expenditure, Julie would feel criticized and away the conflict would go.

Address emotions

Both Jason and Julie had learned in co-counselling how to manage their emotions, and consciously took a step back when they discussed finances. They realized that this was a sensitive subject for each of them and respected that.

Understand each other's positions

They both demonstrated respect for each other's position by listening actively and providing empathy statements to show they had heard the other person. Jason's position was that he:

- was older than Julie
- had aspirations regarding financial balance for the future
- came from a family that was careful with money
- liked to track his income and expenses carefully.

Julie's position was that she:

- had made it on her own before meeting Jason
- hated that financial stuff
- preferred living more spontaneously.

The empathy statement that Jason provided to Julie was 'I understand that you are more flexible than I am with spending.'

The empathy statement that Julie provided to Jason was 'I can see that you have managed your finances carefully for many years, and that my style appears very different from yours.'

Find shared interests

Jason and Julie were very clear about their shared interests:

- commitment to the relationship
- reduced conflict levels
- financial security
- ability to have children within the next two years.

With these shared interests it became easy to move on to generating options.

Explore options

The options they explored were:

- seeing a financial planner
- seeing a marriage counsellor
- Julie taking a course in Quickbooks
- Julie setting up Quickbooks on her computer
- hiring someone to help set up Quickbooks
- John becoming more flexible.

Making a decision

With both partners using subjective decision-making approaches, there was a balanced consideration of the way this subject affected each other. In addition, Julie was deeply committed to Jason (valuing) and Jason hated conflict (harmonizing) so the sooner this area could be addressed the better for both.

They decided to see a marriage counsellor, so that a neutral third party could help them to facilitate a discussion so that this area did not build up. They invested money in having someone set up Quickbooks for Julie, and Jason committed to showing Julie how to use it. Despite the tedious nature of the data entry she has continued to use this to tighten her control over expenses and get them in synch with Jason's. 'I find it really boring, but if that's what it takes I'll do it. I know this will go a long way in making life simpler for us both and it will cut out a lot of fights'. Jason also recognised that he could be less conservative over money, and he focused control over expenditures more on the larger than the smaller items that could give Julie pleasure: a meal out, an outing, etc. _____

Discussion points

1. What does your partner do that angers you? What do you do that angers your partner? What are the sources of conflict in your relationship?

2. To what extent do you use assertive communication when interacting with your partner? When you are stressed, is your preferred style aggressive or submissive? How can you practise using assertive communication?

3. How effective could you be in using the PAUSE technique to resolve conflict? How easy is it for you to see your partner's position? How easy is it for your partner to see your position? To what extent have you been able to focus on shared interests to resolve conflict? How effective are you in generating options based on these shared positions?

4. When you make decisions regarding important aspects of your relationship, to what extent are they joint or individual win/win decisions? What proportion are win/lose? Who tends to be more on the losing side? How could this situation be rectified?

Summary

In this chapter you have learned about the most important steps in managing conflict with your partner:

- ◆ We highlighted the inevitability of conflict in a relationship, and therefore the importance of learning to resolve it successfully.

- ◆ We identified sources of conflict in relationships, these tend to be a mixture of interpersonal and situational factors.

◆ We introduced assertive communication as a tool to express your rights without stepping over your partner's. This win/win interactive style is more likely to result in long-term successful conflict resolution.

◆ You were introduced to the PAUSE technique, a step-by-step approach to resolving conflict. Using this approach will ensure that the conflict does not escalate and the possible solutions are heard by both parties:

  – recognize there is a Problem.
  – Address your and your partner's emotions.
  – Understand your and your partner's positions.
  – focus on Shared interests.
  – Explore options.

◆ Once you have generated options make a decision on future action where both parties win. Trying to make win/win decisions, whether joint or individual, will help to maintain the balance of power in the relationship.

◆ The influence of lovemate and loving styles influences all the above skills and techniques. A greater understanding of our internal wiring can help in managing the conflicts in our relationships.

CHAPTER 8

Relating: Spending Quality Time Together

I n today's busy world one of the most essential factors to a successful partnership is spending quality time together. A couple who cannot play together is unlikely to stay together. However, the pressures on each person's time are considerable, and being able to create time for our partner among the myriad of tasks and conflicting expectations is far from easy. In addition, each partner will vary in terms of the types of activities they enjoy, and how they like to spend their leisure time. Understanding and resolving these issues can help build a positive long-term relationship, and considerably improve each mate's satisfaction with the partnership. This chapter includes exercises to help you and your partner understand your differing expectations around your use of time and explore ways to carve out quality time together.

The pressure of time

> 'I must govern the clock, not be governed by it.'
>
> *Golda Meir.*

According to Charles Handy in *The Age of Paradox*, 'In this turbulent world we never seem to have enough time, yet there has never been so much time.' Life expectancy has risen and technology has reduced the level of manual labour. In addition, specialisation has increased efficiency and output of physical goods and services.

However, two factors appear to be placing increased pressure on the availability of leisure time we can spend in our relationships: more work and more information.

More work

The role of work is shifting in today's economy:

- Work no longer must take place 'at work'. With the presence of technology, people can work anywhere and frequently do – at home, in airports, on planes and on holiday. This reduction of boundaries between the worlds of work and leisure has made it increasingly difficult to ensure dedicated leisure time.

- In addition, work hours are increasing. In the *Overworked American* Juliet Schor identified that in 1992 Americans were working 164 hours more per year than in 1972, and the trend is definitely increasing. Research has shown that we are working approximately two hours more per day and sleeping two hours less per night than we were ten years ago.

More information

In today's high tech economy, the volume and speed of information exchange has increased drastically.

- It seems like only yesterday we were talking about the paper-free society. What a myth! At least with paper we were constrained by the amount we could pile up!

- Instead, we are now deluged by information in all aspects of our life: paper, TV, radio, pagers, cell phones and the Internet. In one daily edition of *The New York Times* there is more information than an individual would receive in an entire year in 19th century England. No longer do we look at encyclopaedias for information, we go to the Web, often to surf through pages and pages of poorly organised information trying to find what we want. This availability of data has created information overload.

- Not only is there more data, the expected exchange of data has increased alarmingly. Ten years ago you would send a letter, and might expect a call within two to three days, or a letter within a week. Today we send an e-mail and expect an instant response. Cell phones, pagers and laptops require us to be instantly available at all times.

> 'Everyone gets so much information all day long that they lose their common sense.'
>
> *Gertrude Stein*

Time for us

Against this backdrop of increased work and information exchange, separating out time for the relationship becomes more and more difficult. Each individual in the partnership has a professional and a personal entity and the partnership is also its own entity. Each entity requires time, humour, communication and creativity. We often neglect the entity of the relationship; many couples find themselves making a bargain of their time for money, hoping that material consumption will give meaning to the relationship and satisfaction to their lives. Unfortunately, it does not work that way.

> 'To keep a lamp burning we have to keep putting oil in it.'
> *Mother Teresa*

Lovemates and the pressure of time

To make the situation even more complex, each lovemate is fundamentally wired to approach this pressure of time differently:

- Playmates thrive on having lots to do, and doing something different every moment. They face the challenge of becoming adrenaline junkies, constantly dashing from one place to another, multiplexing and perhaps neglecting their significant other in the excitement of the moment.
- Helpmates can become overloaded with a constant time pressure, particularly when it is combined with an environment without boundaries. This may cause them to withdraw from their partner as they attempt to institute some structure to the chaos.
- Mindmates can become absorbed in work: work is play and play is work. They will enjoy the challenge of the pressure of time as they attempt to control their destiny. In the process, they may grow more oblivious to their partner's needs and wants as they strive to control the environment.
- Soulmates can be unrealistic with what can actually be achieved, and may find themselves pushing to attain their ideals against the backdrop of this constant time pressure. As a result they may become caught up in their own crisis and miss their partner's need for interaction.

Try it now

How do you respond to time pressure?

Discuss the following questions with your partner.

1. How many hours have you invested in work activities this week and how many has your partner?
2. To what extent are you and your partner able to place boundaries between home and work?
3. What else could you do to protect your time away from work?
4. What communication tools do you both use: cell phone, pager, laptop? To what extent are these tools necessary?
5. Which of these tools could you do without or reduce its use, to create more uninterrupted time for you and your partner?

Prioritizing work/life balance

With this constant pressure of time it is important to be able to prioritize tasks and activities in order to achieve time for our leisure life.

> 'Our life is frittered away by detail . . . simplify, simplify.'
> *Henry David Thoreau*

Whenever we have to prioritize tasks and activities, we need to ask ourselves two critical questions:

1. Is it urgent?
2. Is it important?

From these two questions we can create four quadrants as in Figure 13.

The urgent/important quadrant is called the **quadrant of necessity.** These are tasks and activities that have to be completed on the home and work front. Many of these were listed in the managing reality section in Chapter 5. However, there may be other options for completing these tasks. Many time-crunched couples choose to outsource routine tasks such as grocery shopping, house cleaning, garden maintenance in order to buy themselves time for the other more important quadrants. They trade money for time. This conscious choice can greatly relieve the time pressure on the partnership in two ways:

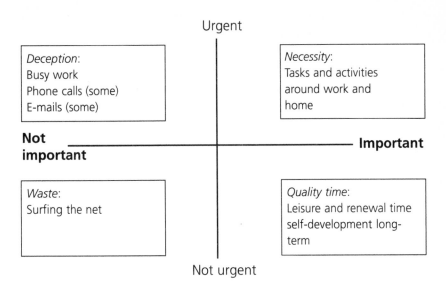

Fig. 13.   Prioritizing work/life.

- ◆ It physically saves time.
- ◆ It takes the weight of responsibility off people's minds, enabling people to feel less overwhelmed by the realities of daily living.

The **urgent/not important quadrant** is called the **quadrant of deception**. We feel we are being productive, but in reality this is 'busy work'. In today's society, responding to the pressure of time, according to Stephen Covey, most of us develop the **urgency habit**. We are constantly running at 100 miles an hour, not necessarily stopping to question the importance of the things we are doing. Types of tasks or activities in this quadrant include:

- Answering the cell phone.
- Returning e-mail messages.
- Other people's crises.

'Most of us start thinking about our work week at 3pm on a Sunday.'

The **important/not urgent quadrant**, the **quadrant of quality time**, covers our developmental interests and is often the quadrant that encompasses our leisure time with our partner. We tend to put this leisure time on the back burner. After all, they are always there, but this work project is critical isn't it?! Unfortunately this often creates problems: either our marriage breaks down, we get sick from overwork, or we forget even how to enjoy leisure time. Our urgency habit destroys our ability to just interact and 'be' with our partner. Types of tasks or activities in this quadrant include:

- Leisurely dinners without interruption.
- Long holidays.
- Long-range planning.
- Defining our values and ground rules.

> 'Most families spend approximately 24 hours of time at weekends on the errands and tasks of daily life.'

The not urgent/not important quadrant, called the **quadrant of waste**, involves tasks and activities that do not need to be done. It includes such things as:

- Surfing the web, just to look around.
- Excessive TV watching.
- Excessive playing of video games.

Here there can often be a fine line between waste and renewal.

Lovemates and prioritizing

Each lovemate tends to prioritize differently:

- Playmates want to do everything and they want to do it now! Long-term tasks, such as those that fit into the quadrant of quality time, may appear too intangible and not as exciting as those in the urgent/not important quadrant. Overcoming the urgency habit can be of great benefit to playmates in all aspects of their life.
- Helpmates will approach prioritizing in a logical, step-by-step manner. However, with their developed sense of responsibility they may be reluctant to let go in the quadrant of necessity, in order to delegate tasks and activities to others. They may also struggle with allowing themselves time for the quadrant of quality time, if activity there appears too abstract or frivolous.
- Mindmates will approach prioritizing from a logical, analytical perspective, weighing the pros and cons of different activities.

However, with their lack of awareness of detailed logistical implementation, they may underestimate time or energy required for tasks. In setting priorities they may not provide the people factor with adequate emphasis.

◆ Soulmates will approach prioritization from the perspective of people and the relative importance of the factors relating to their purpose and cause. As such, they may devalue or be unaware of the practical tasks and activities that need to be completed. They may need to achieve a balance between working in their interest areas and working with their partner, within the quadrant of quality time.

Try it now

Prioritizing tasks and activities

Refer back to the quadrants in Figure 13.

Step 1: Individually list the tasks and activities that you complete on a weekly basis.

Step 2: Now individually assign the tasks to the quadrant in which you believe they belong.

Step 3: Discuss the following questions with your partner.

◆ Were you in agreement with which tasks were assigned to the quadrant of necessity? Which of these tasks could you accomplish more effectively or delegate?

◆ To what extent do each of you run on the urgency habit? What can you do to reduce your propensity for running on adrenaline?

◆ How can you ensure you allocate time for the important/not urgent quadrant: for quality time? What tasks or activities that fit in this quadrant will you begin this week? This month?

◆ What tasks or activities will you try to eliminate from the not urgent/not important quadrant?

Understanding leisure time

For most of the history of civilization, couples and families spent days working together. Now work tends to separate partners, and leisure time is the activity that is supposed to reconnect couples. The whole concept of leisure time has taken on a new meaning.

> 'Leisure is the heartland of contemporary couple relationships.'
> *Polly Young-Eisendrath*

However, leisure time is very unstructured, and an area for which we often do not consider structure or approach – that's why it's called leisure time! People tend to evaluate the worth of their relationship more in terms of the pleasure that is shared in leisure (companionship) than in terms of other concerns – sex, kids, money, etc. This facet, combined with long work hours, increase the expectations and significance of leisure time. In other words, not only do we have less time, and we are more tired, we now expect our leisure time to be even better to compensate for the first two factors. A double whammy!

> 'We both work very hard right now and cherish our free time. When we have a weekend the only thing we want to do is spend time together.'
> On joint leisure time

Leisure time can be looked at in several ways. The first is by considering interactive, passive and separate activities.

Interactive activities

Interactive activities normally involve communication and direct sharing of the experience. Spending time with your partner in interactive activities has proved to be beneficial for the quality of the relationship. Interactive activities include such things as:
- Having dinner together (as long as you are talking, and not reading books or speaking on cell phones!).
- Travelling together (with the same caveats!).
- Discussing issues, whether political, social, economical, etc.
- Going to a museum or art gallery together and discussing art and culture.

Passive activities

Passive activities involve partners doing something together which does not involve much interaction. Passive activity creates the illusion of togetherness even though you are not. The relationship does not develop and neither do the people in it. One day you wake up and wonder who the other person is. Passive activities tend to have little or no benefit to the partnership because there is limited quality interaction, although they may be important for the individual to renew him or herself occasionally. Passive activities include such things as:

◆ Watching TV (unless you are discussing it extensively afterwards).
◆ Watching movies (with the same qualification factor).
◆ Going to a show.

Separate activities

Separate activities are those that each partner completes alone. These types of activities may fulfil a specific need, which lead to individual happiness and a better disposition in the relationship as a result. The factor that influences their effect on the partnership is dependent on what the other partner feels is acceptable. If your partner thinks time spent on these activities is too much, then they may have a negative effect on the relationship and result in separation anxiety. On the other hand, if they are viewed to be in alignment with your partner's expectations, and they provide stimulus for the joint activities, they may build a stronger relationship.

> 'My trip was something I needed to do by myself before we were married. It fulfilled a dream I have always had. My partner and I discussed the separation seriously and agreed on five months volunteering in Central America versus two years in the Peace Corps. We were very confident in the strength of our partnership despite physical distance between us.'
>
> Soulmate discussing taking a trip without her mindmate partner

Separate activities include such things as:
◆ Going to workshops separately.
◆ Going to sports events with buddies.
◆ Reading.
◆ Shopping alone.
◆ Taking a trip.

Influence of temperament

As each temperament approaches the pressure of time differently, so they also enjoy different facets of leisure time. Broadly both playmates and mindmates tend to be pragmatic in the use of their time: will do what it takes, and may be perceived by their mate to be less caring about the relationship. Helpmates and soulmates tend to be collaborative around relationships: they naturally consider the people involved. However, their approach should not be correlated with a judgement pertaining to caring. All temperaments care, they simply approach the situation in a different way.

- Playmates tend to get involved in a variety of tactile projects and/or sports for leisure. In addition they tend to have no clearly defined hierarchy in personal priorities – whatever is at hand is the focus of attention. They are likely to enjoy spending leisure time in outdoor activities or playing with the latest cool toys and tools.

- Helpmates tend to use their leisure time looking after the hearth and home and they enjoy the routine of family life. They enjoy tactile hobbies such as fixing cars and equipment, and may be involved in community activities. They are talented in scheduling social rituals and gatherings, but they may also become overloaded with family responsibilities.

- Mindmates, once they are married, may go back to their usual separate interests, and appear to give more attention to interests than to their mate and sometimes appear to neglect the marital maintenance arena. They enjoy debating issues, so may indulge in interactive activities that involve discussion around points of interest. Their strong sense of independence may cause them to resist too many interactive shared activities.

- Soulmates may have difficulty separating themselves from their personal involvements to focus on their partner, particularly if their partner's interests revolve around concrete reality instead of abstract possibilities. On the other hand, if they have no current cause or mission, they may find it difficult to separate from their partner and instead become absorbed in the relationship. They will normally try to get their mate interested in their latest passion, whether it is self-development, yoga, or gourmet cooking.

'We love cooking and eating, travelling, many sports, reading, music, and spending time with friends and certain family members. I like spending time with my girlfriends and I have a lot of artistic creative pursuits apart from John. He swims, runs, gardens and sees friends. He sometimes goes away for the weekend to workshops.'

Playmate and soulmate describing how they spend their leisure time.

Try it now

How we spend our time

1. List all the activities you do together in a week (eg in the past week).
2. Categorize each of the activities according to:
   – interactive
   – passive
   – separate.

Talk it through

◆ How well do you do in terms of spending quality, interactive time together?

◆ To what extent did you engage in passive activities? How much did you use these activities for stimulating discussion? How could you reduce the amount of passive activities?

◆ How much time did you spend separate from each other? How much of that time did the person 'left behind' think was reasonable and fair?

◆ How did you see your partner's temperament in the types of activities they enjoyed?

Understanding gender differences

As we discussed in Chapter 3, Valuing Differences, gender differences can also influence the way we approach our leisure time.

◆ The use of 'report' talk versus 'rapport' talk will influence the quality of our interactive activities. If the female is communicating to make a connection and discuss feelings while the male is wanting to fix the issue and give data, the interaction is not likely to be as positive as it could be.

♦ Studies conducted by Polly Young-Eisendrath, described in *You're Not What I Expected*, have shown that men tend to enjoy watching TV in the evenings and at the weekends. Females appeared to share the interest during the week; at weekends there appears to be a conflict between women wanting to converse and men wanting to watch the TV.

♦ In leisure time another significant difference between women and men appears to be in the type of active and passive interests they enjoy.

 – Women tend to enjoy reading as a passive interest and communicating with their partner as their active endeavour.

 – Men tend to watch TV as their passive interest and sports as their active pursuit.

♦ If we are not careful this can create further divisions between the partners as their active and passive leisure interests are different.

♦ Couples whose relationship has stood the test of time have normally reached an agreement, whether consciously or by chance, about how they spend their leisure time.

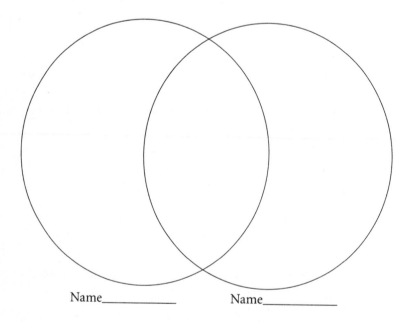

Name_____   Name_____

Fig. 14. Venn diagram.

Try it now

What are your interests?

Make a copy of the Venn diagram in Figure 14.

1. Label each of the non-overlapping areas of the Venn diagram with your names (one name on each side).
2. In the portion of the circles that overlap, list your mutual areas of interest: activities, sports, hobbies, etc.
3. In the part of the diagram that you labelled with your name, list your areas of individual interest. Have your partner do the same thing for his/her section.

Talk it through

- Are your areas of shared and independent interests balanced?
- Which of your partner's activities/interests could you enjoy together? How could you make the activity fun for both of you?
- To what extent could you take on one of your partner's interests?
- How could you better balance your interests to capitalize on your leisure time together? How much of that time would you be doing what you wanted to do, versus what your partner wanted to do?

Spending holidays together

> 'I think we get along much better on vacation without the everyday household and work responsibilities.'
>
> Helpmate describing a holiday

One of the most concentrated interactive types of times that a couple spends together is holidays. Unfortunately time allocated for holidays can be lost to the pressure of work. It's worth stating, however, that older people when reflecting back on their past rarely say 'What a great project', rather they will remember time with loved ones. Holidays provide couples with either the opportunity to connect or divide. Couples who have a successful long-term relationship find that uninterrupted holidays can provide them with time to regroup and renew, discuss important issues, share new experiences and reconnect as a couple. For couples who find taking holidays together stressful, other opportunities can be explored to create quality interactive time, such as sharing an interest, taking up a hobby, etc.

Lovemates can also be attracted to different holidays However, even if what is enriching to one is different for the other, the couple can still spend quality time together.

> 'Nepal, we almost died together: fun, sex, crime, rats, killer monkeys, non-stop Indiana Jones.'
>
> Playmate describing his favourite vacation in Nepal
>
> 'My favourite vacation was going to Nepal on a trek: the combination of a simple, spiritually based culture, physical endurance, the magnificent outdoors and the most gentle and kind people, really had a profound effect on us.'
>
> Soulmate describing the same vacation

Deciding who will chose a location, who will plan holidays, and ensuring that holidays are regularly scheduled can help energise the partnership on an ongoing basis.

Case Studies

In this case study we look at two couples as they approach sharing quality time together. Again they approached their leisure time very differently based on their temperament and loving style. The profiles of the two couples are below.

Personality	Sheila and Brian		Andrew and Christine	
	Helpmate	**Playmate**	**Mindmate**	**Soulmate**
Information-gathering	Recalling	Experiencing	Brainstorming	Brainstorming
Decision-making	Harmonizing	Analyzing	Analyzing	Valuing
Direction of energy	Extroverting	Introverting	Extroverting	Introverting
Loving style	Extroverted nurturer	Introverted manoeuvrer	Extroverted inventor or innovator	Introverted advocate

Prioritizing and pressure of time

Sheila and Brian both work full-time and have two children. To carve out some leisure time they have both made certain decisions on things not to do. They decided to hire an agency to do the housework because, although it had to be done, there were other resources that could do it. This was difficult for Sheila: as a helpmate she felt it was her responsibility to do this, and Brian had to highlight the more important role she could play with her children instead in the extra time available. Brian tried to limit his time playing computer games. While it was relaxing to an extent, he realised that taking it to excess was counterproductive.

Andrew and Christine had no children. Andrew was in Law School and Christine was working full-time for a consulting company. When they prioritised their time, the fact that Christine travelled constantly made it very difficult to complete all the activities in the quadrant of important and urgent, not to mention the key relationship activities of important/not urgent. Andrew was engrossed in his studies and the social life of a student. He sometimes felt single again, as Christine was only there at weekends. They lived in complete disarray. After over a year trying to establish a better balance, she decided to look for another position which did not have such a negative effect on their quality of life.

Leisure time

When Sheila and Brian completed the grid highlighting interactive, passive and separate time, the results were as listed below.

Interactive	Passive	Separate
Before bed talk	TV	Bike
	Volleyball	Exercise
	Movie	House chores
		Read
		Go out with friends
		Time with kids
		Tinker
5%	5%	90%

As with many couples with children, their quality interactive time as a couple was extremely limited. They realised that if they wanted to make sure that when the children grew up a partnership still existed between them, they would have to change this balance. They instituted a date night once a week and decided to revisit the prioritising grid to see if any other activities could be delegated. You could really see the helpmate's skills as Sheila focused on decorating, room layout and gardening. Her talents were a great contributing factor in building a nest.

When Andrew and Christine reviewed their exercise of activities (see Figure 15) it served as an affirmation of the characteristics that had drawn them together in the first place. There were many abstract subjects that they enjoyed discussing with each other. What was revealed was that Andrew's interest in sports (not uncommon for men) consumed a great deal of time. They decided to take two actions:

1. Christine picked out Andrew's favourite sport, football, and decided to learn more about it.
2. Andrew decided to moderate his sports activities so that they did not interfere with their time together.

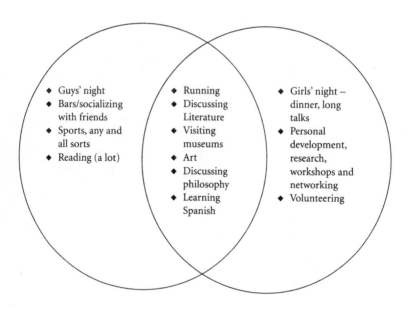

Fig. 15.   Sample Venn diagram: Andrew and Christine.

3. They tried to co-ordinate their schedules to do more of their running together – a sport they mutually enjoyed.

Taking holidays together

Both couples enjoyed taking holidays together. Sheila enjoyed organizing and taking family trips, the entire extended family would participate. They would use these times away to try different things together. Sheila did research to get the best deal in their travels. Brian would sometimes irritate her on these trips, because he was much more free spending! He loved to try new food and scouring the shops for local artifacts, which accounted for a lot of their expenditure. Many of the dinner conversations revolved around memories of other special occasions. On bank holidays Sheila would ensure that tradition was celebrated: Christmas carols, decorating and baking, creating themes for special days, etc.

By contrast, Christine and Andrew loved to travel to new places together, where the experience of the event was less important than the discussion that it stimulated: Andrew from putting a tick in the box that he had learned something new, Christine from learning about humanity. They would then enjoy discussing the greater issues such as what could be learned from each culture and way of life.

At the end of specific celebrations such as graduating, the beginning of the new millennium, etc they would discuss the greater patterns or themes around the event: what does the beginning of the new century really mean? What will their future life be like? How can they fulfil their dreams against the forces of reality? What personal fulfilment would be the best for both of them? Making decisions about time together was often hard because neither of them enjoyed organizing the tactical steps, and with their future focus they often forgot concrete reality. _____

Discussion points

1. To what extent are you and your partner sensitive to the pressure of time? How easy is it for you to differentiate between home and work? How much do you feel you have to respond instantly to the many types of information you receive?

2. When discussing prioritizing, to what extent to you run on the urgency habit? How can you ensure you make time for activities in the quadrant of quality time? What tasks or activities could you delegate to free up some time and reduce

the day-to-day pressure?

3. When you consider your activities, to what extent are they interactive? Which are separate? What percentage of your time do you spend on passive activities? How could you realign your activities to greater effect?

4. When you consider the gender differences, to what extent are your active interests similar? How could you combine or share more of these? What about your passive interests such as reading, watching sports, etc? How could you combine or share more of these?

Summary

In this chapter we have reviewed the importance of leisure time as a critical factor influencing the satisfaction that each partner feels with the relationship. We discussed:

- Today partners struggle with placing boundaries around the never-ending world of work and the deluge of information they are bombarded with daily.

- Faced with this increasing time pressure, the only way that couples can make time for each other is if they prioritize between the things that are really important and those that are not. Many of us act in the moment, completing tasks that are not important, because of the pressure of the urgency habit. In addition, many of us do not review unnecessary tasks and activities or those that could be delegated to others, to enable us to spend time with our significant other in the quadrant of quality time.

- Once we have prioritized in this way we need to consider the way we spend time with our partner, whether it is in interactive, passive or separate activities. Increasing the time spent in interactive activities, those that require joint communication, is the greatest influence on the perceived success of the relationship. It produces a feeling of companionship.

- We also have to ensure that the differences in gender preferences between the types of active and passive interests do not divide our partnership further. If we can share more active interests, we will feel more satisfied in our relationship.

- Finally, our whole approach to time is influenced by our

temperament: understanding how our partner may view leisure time differently from us can help to eliminate boundaries and build the basis for positive leisure time together.

It is good to
have an end to
journey
towards; but it
is the journey
that matters in
the end.

SUMMARY

Keeping the Passion Alive

A s you have seen in your journey through this book, building a sustainable long-term relationship requires energy, flexibility and commitment. What's more, the process is never complete: it needs continuous effort and involvement. Faced with the challenges of managing to do this against the backdrop of daily reality, many couples give up and move onto another partnership, only to find they face the same issues there.

> 'Pay attention. Listen. Don't criticise. Touch a lot. Pick up treats, books, etc which the other person is interested in. Always kiss/hug hello and goodbye. Talk a lot. Don't nit-pick over nits. Cuddle almost every morning and night. Give foot rubs and back rubs. Speak to each other and about each other positively. Accept the other's foibles with affection not sufferance.'
>
> On keeping the passion alive

However, when you look at the advice of the couple above, it's really not rocket science and the benefits are enormous. You have made the first step in maintaining a rewarding relationship by buying this book. Continuing to practise the skills and techniques introduced here will help your relationship survive and thrive far into the new millennium. Good luck.

Loving style descriptions

LOVING STYLE	EXTROVERTED MANOEUVRER: *Love is an adventure*	
Temperament	**Playmate:**	To act in the moment, be noticed and produce immediate concrete tangible results.
Direction of energy	**Extroverting:**	Energy goes outwards: process externally and show more obvious body language.
First function	**Experiencing:**	Rapid uptake of sensory data in the now from the external world. Acute awareness of specifics and realities in the world around them.
Second function	**Analyzing:**	Make decisions using their internal logical criteria and principles. Analyze how and why things work.
Shadow function	**Harmonizing:**	Aware of subjective criteria to optimize group interaction.
Shadow function	**Visioning:**	Occasionally gather information by creating their own complete idea or future direction. Verify with sensory data.
Description	**Extroverted Manoeuvrers:** Action-oriented, quick thinking, quick moving, objective decision-makers. Their focus on making things happen can make them appear impatient with slow-moving, theoretical discussion and concepts. Direct, to the point, their word choice focuses on 'netting it out'. They possess intense observation skills, can tune in to what's happening in the moment, are acutely aware of non-verbal cues and then respond as needed. Their minds move so quickly that often their words are left behind, as they push on to closure. They constantly find new ways of doing things. Sometimes perceived as uncaring by their partners, they nonetheless protect the people who are important to them.	

LOVING STYLE	INTROVERTED MANOEUVRERS: *Love is a game*	
Temperament	**Playmate:**	To act in the moment, be noticed and produce immediate concrete tangible results.
Direction of energy	**Introverting:**	Energy goes inwards: tend to process and reflect, don't see all emotions.
First function	**Analyzing:**	Make decisions using their internal logical criteria and principles. Analyze how and why things work.
Second function	**Experiencing:**	Rapid uptake of sensory data in the now from the external world. Acute awareness of specifics and realities in the world around them.
Shadow function	**Visioning:**	Occasionally gather information by creating their own complete idea or future direction. Verify with sensory data.
Shadow function	**Harmonizing**	Aware of subjective criteria to optimize group interaction.
Description	**Introverted manoeuvrers** live in the present and act in the moment to get to the root cause and solve problems. They are the most analytical of the playmates, enjoying theoretical constructs with practical reasoning. They can absorb huge amounts of impersonal facts and have a high affiliation with numbers. They thrive on variety and focus on doing what needs to be done with the least amount of fuss. They will change direction readily as additional information becomes available, and manoeuvre systems to meet their ends. They are adept with tools and able to reason impersonally and objectively. They may alienate their partner with their apparent manipulation, but then love is a game to them.	

LOVING STYLE	EXTROVERTED IMPROVIZER: *Love is a performance*	
Temperament	**Playmate:**	To act in the moment, be noticed and produce immediate concrete tangible results.
Direction of energy	**Extroverting:**	Energy goes outwards: process externally and show more obvious body language.
First function	**Experiencing:**	Rapid uptake of sensory data in the now from the external world. Acute awareness of

		specifics and realities in the world around them.
Second function	**Valuing:**	Make decisions quietly, but firmly based on their own internal beliefs system. Guided by strong inner values and wish life to be in congruence with those beliefs.
Shadow function	**Systematizing:**	Will make some decisions using logical criteria to plan and organize logistics and events in the external world.
Shadow function	**Visioning:**	Will occasionally gather information by creating their own complete idea or future direction. Will verify with sensory data.
Description	**Extroverted improvizers**: are colourful, free-spirited and people-focused. Using their acute sensory inputs they make decisions based on what is in alignment with their internal values system. They are interested in people and new experiences, as they live in the moment. They are generous of spirit, active, talkative and flexible. Their natural exuberance attracts others as they get the task done with the maximum amount of fun and minimum amount of fuss. They find enjoyment in food, clothes, animals, the natural world and activities. They work best in a flexible, unstructured environment. They are fun-loving, however their tendency to perform in groups and see the light-hearted side may make their partner want them to be more serious.	

LOVING STYLE	INTROVERTED IMPROVIZER: *Love and be happy*	
Temperament	**Playmate:**	To act in the moment, be noticed, and produce immediate, concrete, tangible results.
Direction of energy	**Introverting:**	Energy goes inwards: tend to process and reflect, don't see all emotions.
First function	**Valuing:**	Makes decisions quietly, but firmly based on their own internal beliefs system. Guided by strong inner values and wish life to be in congruence with those beliefs.
Second function	**Experiencing:**	Rapid uptake of sensory data in the now from the external world. Acute awareness of

		specifics and realities in the world around them.
Shadow function	**Visioning:**	Occasionally gather information by creating their own complete idea or future direction. Verify with sensory data.
Shadow function	**Systematizing:**	Make some decisions using logical criteria to plan and organise logistics and events in the external world.
Description		**Introverted improvizers** live in the present and prize the freedom to follow their own course. They are faithful at fulfilling obligations to people and things that are important to them. They often appear as unassuming, easy-going, gentle and soft-spoken. They provide help in concrete, tangible ways, and with their observation skills have a gift of expressing abstract things concretely. Their playful sense of humour may not be seen until they are comfortable with you. They adapt well to new situations and approach life from a 'don't worry be happy' perspective. In relationships their tendency to be laid back in their approach could be viewed as lack of interest or direction.

LOVING STYLE	EXTROVERTED NURTURER: *Creating a loving framework*	
Temperament	**Helpmate:**	To be part of a group or a team, fulfil responsibilities and make a contribution therein.
Direction of energy	**Extroverting:**	Energy goes outwards: process externally and show more obvious body language.
First function	**Harmonizing:**	Making decisions using subjective criteria to optimize group harmony.
Second function	**Recalling:**	Gather information by referring to a rich databank of past sensory experiences and comparing and contrasting with the present.
Shadow function	**Brainstorming:**	Some external exploration of future possibilities, patterns and meaning based on building on historic data.
Shadow function	**Analyzing:**	May compare and contrast data against an internal model, but this will be superseded by appropriateness to the group.

Description	Extroverted nurturers are warm, personable and outgoing. They enjoy harmonious relationship environments, working within that structure to ensure organization is established and responsibilities are met. They are conscientious and loyal, and value security and stability. They use information from their extensive databank of past sensory experiences to apply in their concrete, task-focused work. They are energized by being with others and are genuinely interested in others' lives and concerns. They enjoy participating in committees and are good at organizing celebrations and preserving traditions. As partners, they will be the organiser of all family celebrations, yet may sometimes overload themselves with family responsibilities.

LOVING STYLE	INTROVERTED NURTURER: *Comforting each other*	
Temperament	**Helpmate:**	To be part of a group or a team, fulfil responsibilities and make a contribution therein.
Direction of energy	**Introverting:**	Energy goes inwards: tend to process and reflect, don't see all emotions.
First function	**Recalling:**	Gather information by referring to a rich databank of past sensory experiences, and comparing and contrasting with the present.
Second function	**Harmonizing:**	Making decisions using subjective criteria to optimize group harmony.
Shadow function	**Analyzing:**	May compare and contrast data against an internal model, but this will be superseded by appropriateness to the group.
Shadow function	**Brainstorming:**	Some external exploration of future possibilities, patterns and meaning based on building on historic data.
Description	Introverted nurturers are stable, supportive, empathetic partners who look after house and home. They are concrete, task-focused, and value possessions and economy of resources. Valuing traditions and historic experience, they make decisions that will meet the needs of the group. When communicating they follow a detailed, sequential, step-by-step thought process and tend to establish orderly procedures. They enjoy helping others, are dependable and considerate,	

and gravitate to roles that involve service to others. Maintaining the cohesiveness of the relationship and living up to their responsibilities are fundamental to the way they operate. As partners they have to be careful that they are not taken advantage of, because they will do tasks for others in such an unassuming way the effort goes unnoticed.

LOVING STYLE	EXTROVERTED REGULATORS: *'til death us do part*	
Temperament	**Helpmate:**	To be part of a group or a team, fulfil responsibilities and make a contribution therein.
Direction of energy	**Extroverting:**	Energy goes outwards: process externally and show more obvious body language.
First function	**Systematizing:**	Making decisions using logical criteria to plan and organise logistics and events in the external world.
Second function	**Recalling:**	Gather information by referring to a rich databank of past sensory experiences and comparing and contrasting with the present.
Shadow function	**Brainstorming:**	Some external exploration of future possibilities, patterns and meaning based on building on historic data.
Shadow function	**Valuing:**	May consider their internal values and beliefs, but this decision will be subservient to logical criteria.
Description	**Extroverted regulators** are detail-oriented, high-energy decision-makers. They drive for closure with the aim of organizing, planning and structuring the external environment. The most 'driven' of the helpmates, they take action to get things done, in a systematic and consistent way. They take an objective approach to problem-solving and can be tough when the situation demands. They enjoy activity that produces concrete tangible results and are adept at creating systems that assign responsibilities and marshal resources. They enjoy interacting with others, especially around games and family activities. As partners they set high standards and have a clear internal barometer of right and wrong.	

LOVING STYLE	INTROVERTED REGULATORS: *Taking the right steps together*	
Temperament	**Helpmate:**	To be part of a group or a team, fulfil responsibilities and make a contribution therein.
Direction of energy	**Introverting:**	Energy goes inwards: tends to process and reflect, don't see all emotions.
First function	**Recalling:**	Gather information by referring to a rich databank of past sensory experiences and comparing and contrasting with the present.
Second function	**Systematizing:**	Making decisions using logical criteria to plan and organise logistics and events in the external world.
Shadow function	**Valuing:**	May consider their internal values and beliefs, but this decision will be subservient to logical criteria.
Shadow function	**Brainstorming:**	Some external exploration of future possibilities, patterns and meaning based on building on historic data.
Description	**Introverted regulators** are logical, practical, organized and thorough. They rely on historic experience from which to create concrete action plans. They will create processes and procedures to smooth work flow, eliminate redundancy and achieve economy of effort. They are loyal and dutiful, and work with steady energy to ensure commitments are met on time. They tend to prefer to have time alone and may appear serious and orderly. They trust facts, are task-oriented and can manage extensive detail. They work hard at whatever they do and once a skill is learned, perform it with competence. As partners they are dedicated and committed but may frustrate their mate in their sequential, one thing at a time, approach.	

LOVING STYLE	EXTROVERTED MARSHALLER: *We will make love work*	
Temperament	**Mindmate:**	To be competent and knowledgeable and to understand the universal operating principles in order to create their own destiny.
Direction of energy	**Extroverting:**	Energy goes outwards: process externally and show more obvious body language.
First function	**Systematizing:**	Making decisions using logical criteria to

		plan and organise logistics and events in the external world.
Second function	**Visioning:**	Gather information by creating their own complete idea or future direction.
Shadow function	**Experiencing:**	May observe and gather sensory data as a support to the future picture.
Shadow function	**Valuing:**	May consider their internal values and beliefs, but this decision will be subservient to logical criteria.
Description	**Extroverted marshallers** are direct, organised and possess a strong desire to make their inner visions a reality. They are quick-thinking, strategic, logical decision-makers, possessing a drive for closure. They value intelligence or competence and abhor inefficiency. They conceptualize and theorize readily and possess the innate ability to take charge and make things happen. They exude confidence and appear energetic and driven. They are aware of intricate connections that they can explain with a logical model. As partners they want to ensure that a relationship is working efficiently, and may appear uncomfortable with too many emotional issues.	

LOVING STYLE	INTROVERTED MARSHALLER: *Love is viewed independently*	
Temperament	**Mindmate:**	To be competent and knowledgeable and to understand universal operating principles in order to create their own destiny.
Direction of energy	**Introverting:**	Energy goes inwards: tend to process and reflect, don't see all emotions.
First function	**Visioning:**	Gather information by creating their own complete idea or future direction.
Second function	**Systematizing:**	Making decisions using logical criteria to plan and organise logistics and events in the external world.
Shadow function	**Valuing:**	May consider their internal values and beliefs, but this decision will be subservient to logical criteria.
Shadow function	**Experiencing:**	May observe and gather sensory data as a support to the future picture.
Description	**Introverted marshallers** approach life with an independent-minded long-term vision coming from their internal world of	

possibilities. They make concrete tangible action plans to achieve their overall objectives. They can always offer a detached, objective perspective with the propensity for original thought as they see patterns in external events. With their ability to categorize data, they are confident in their ideas and their ability to achieve their goals. They can appear determined as they strive to achieve their high standards of performance. As partners they may not reveal their inner emotions, but they can be strongly loyal mates and can always be relied upon for an independent opinion.

LOVING STYLE	EXTROVERTED INNOVATORS: *Love is a puzzle to be solved*	
Temperament	**Mindmate:**	To be competent and knowledgeable and to understand universal operating principles in order to create their own destiny.
Direction of energy	**Extroverting:**	Energy goes outwards: process externally and show more obvious body language.
First function	**Brainstorming:**	Constant external exploration of future possibilities, patterns and meaning.
Second function	**Analyzing:**	Make decisions using internal logical criteria and principles. Analyze how and why things work. Evaluate and sort against an internal mental model.
Shadow function	**Harmonizing:**	Aware of subjective criteria to optimize group interaction.
Shadow function	**Recalling:**	May go back to historic data, but may project negative past experiences into the future.
Description	**Extroverted innovators** are normally quick-thinking, verbally expressive and always focused on future opportunities. They thrive on looking at concepts and possibilities from multiple angles and then arguing their own philosophy or hypothesis. They are optimistic, gregarious and social. they enjoy debate and can be very persuasive. They naturally generate options and then are able to analyze them strategically, which makes them creative, abstract problem solvers. They are enterprising and resourceful, however they may have difficulty in the implementation of the idea. As partners they will be upbeat, enthusiastic mates, however their need	

| | to take centre stage and challenge others' viewpoints could wear down those around them. |

LOVING STYLE	INTROVERTED INNOVATORS: *Love is a work in progress*	
Temperament	**Mindmate:**	To be competent and knowledgeable and to understand universal operating principles in order to create their own destiny.
Decision of energy	**Introverting:**	Energy goes inwards: tend to process and reflect, don't see all emotions.
First function	**Analyzing:**	Make decisions using internal logical criteria and principles. Analyze how and why things work. Evaluate and sort against an internal mental model.
Second function	**Brainstorming:**	Constant external exploration of future possibilities, patterns and meaning.
Shadow function	**Recalling:**	May go back to historic data, but may project negative past experiences into the future.
Shadow function	**Harmonizing:**	Aware of subjective criteria to optimize group interaction.
Description	**Introverted innovators** spend their lives in a quest for logical purity. Using abstract data from ideas, future possibilities and meanings, they analyze this information to align with their internal models. They possess an insight into complex theories and constantly search for patterns and systems to internally categorize data. They often function autonomously as they absorb themselves in mastering and perfecting their theories. They possess a unique ability to dissect the complex and comprehend conceptual subtleties. They enjoy creating conceptual solutions but then may struggle with their implementation, as they live in their rich inner world. As partners they may appear distanced from the real world.	

LOVING STYLE	EXTROVERTED ACTUALIZERS: *The relationship is everything*	
Temperament	**Soulmate:**	To have a purpose and make a meaningful contribution to the greater good: helping people to develop.
Direction of energy	**Extroverting:**	Energy goes outwards: process externally and show more obvious body language.
First function	**Harmonizing:**	Making decisions using subjective criteria to optimize group interaction.
Second function	**Visioning:**	Gather information by creating their own complete idea or future direction.
Shadow function	**Experiencing:**	May observe and gather sensory data as a support to the future picture.
Shadow function	**Analyzing:**	May compare and contrast data against an internal model, but this will be superseded by appropriateness to the group.
Description	**Extroverted actualizers:** are outgoing, empathetic, expressive developers of people. They have a remarkable gift of seeing human potential and want to help others be all that they can be. With their long-term focus, they like closure in their lives as they work to make their visions a reality. They are gifted communicators whether one-to-one, where they are able to get almost anyone to open up to them, or in front of a group where they are able to stimulate a positive enthusiasm. They are highly attuned to the moods and emotions of those around them, and work to create a harmonious environment. As partners they focus on meaningful communication in the relationship, and drive to create genuine interactions with their mates and offspring. However, their focus on their cause could detract from the relationship.	

LOVING STYLE	INTROVERTED ACTUALIZERS: *There are happy endings*	
Temperament	**Soulmate:**	To have a purpose and make a meaningful contribution to the greater good: helping people to develop.
Direction of energy	**Introverting:**	Energy goes inwards: tend to process and reflect, don't see all emotions.

First function	Visioning:	Gather information by creating their own complete idea or future direction.
Second function	Harmonizing:	Making decisions using subjective criteria to optimize group interaction.
Shadow function	Analyzing:	May compare and contrast data against an internal model, but this will be superseded by appropriateness to the group.
Shadow function	Experiencing:	May observe and gather sensory data as a support to the future picture.
Description		**Introverted actualizers** are quietly insightful individuals who are constantly searching for deeper meanings and the coming into consciousness of their inner visions. They empathetically understand the feelings and motivations of others and are loyal to people and institutions. As tactful, thoughtful and concerned individuals they demonstrate interest in the development of others. They are very private people, they quietly exert an influence over others. They use language that is full of imagery as they structure the external world to work towards their inner picture of the future. As partners they will be sensitive to their mate's emotional issues on their constant quest to make their vision a reality. However, their drive to achieve their vision may not be tempered with reality.

LOVING STYLE	EXTROVERTED ADVOCATES: *Be with me*	
Temperament	Soulmate:	To have a purpose and make a meaningful contribution to the greater good: helping people to develop.
Direction of energy	Extroverting:	Energy goes outwards: process externally and show more obvious body language.
First function	Brainstorming:	Constant external exploration of future possibilities, patterns and meanings.
Second function	Valuing:	Make decisions quietly, but firmly based on their own internal beliefs system. Guided by strong inner values and wish life to be in congruence with those.
Shadow function	Systematizing:	Make some decisions using logical criteria to plan and organise logistics and events in the external world.

Shadow function	**Recalling:**	May go back to historic data, but may project negative past experiences into the future.
Description	**Extroverted advocates**	are energetic, spontaneous, warm-hearted individuals who constantly generate creative ingenious options for the future. They see endless possibilities that relate to the people around them. They love abstract concepts and are able to see beyond the obvious to the hidden meanings and patterns. Their strong inner values guide their decision-making, as they readily give appreciation and support to others. They are empathetic and engaging, keenly perceptive of others, and use their verbal fluency to persuade and influence those around them. As partners they are enthusiastic and committed to the relationships that are important to them, although they may frustrate their partner with their lack of concrete focus.

LOVING STYLE	INTROVERTED ADVOCATES: *I believe in love*	
Temperament	**Soulmate:**	To have a purpose and make a meaningful contribution to the greater good: helping people to develop.
Direction of energy	**Introverting:**	Energy goes inwards: tend to process and reflect, don't see all emotions.
First function	**Valuing:**	Make decisions quietly, but firmly based on their own internal beliefs system. Guided by strong inner values and wish life to be in congruence with those.
Second function	**Brainstorming:**	Constant external exploration of future possibilities, patterns and meanings.
Shadow function	**Recalling:**	May go back to historic data, but may project negative past experiences into the future.
Shadow function	**Systematizing:**	Make some decisions using logical criteria to plan and organise logistics and events in the external world.
Description	**Introverted advocates**	are quiet pursuers of their life's quest as they strive to live according to their strongly held internal values. Not wanting to take centre stage, they can appear reserved and somewhat aloof until their internal belief

system is bumped up against, when they can react strongly in its defence. With a moral commitment to the fundamental worth of unique identity, they celebrate individual differences and want a purpose beyond a paycheck. They are adaptable, and enjoy opportunities to explore the complexities of human personality. They value relationships based on authenticity and true connection. However, they may frustrate their partner with their constant push to live life according to their own internal ideals.

Further Reading

TYPE AND TEMPERAMENT BOOKS

Turning Team Performance Inside Out, Susan Nash (Davies Black 1999).

Please Understand Me, David Keirsey and Marilyn Bates (Del Mar: Prometheus Nemesis Books 1978).

Please Understand Me II, David Keirsey (Del Mar: Prometheus Nemesis Books, 1998).

Gifts Differing, Isabel Briggs Myers and Peter B Myers (Palo Alto: Consulting Psychologists Press, Inc., 1980).

Portraits of Temperament, David Keirsey (Del Mar Prometheus Nemesis Books 1987).

Beside Ourselves: Our Hidden Personality in Everyday Life, Naomi Quenk (Davies Black Publishing 1993).

Life Types, Sandra Hirsh and Jean Kummerow (New York: Warner Books, Inc 1989).

It Takes All Types, Alan W. Brownsword (Baytree Publication Company 1994).

Survival Games Personalities Play, Eve Delunas (Sunflower, Inc. 1992).

Type Talk, Otto Kroeger and Janet M. Thuesen (New York: Delacorte Press 1988).

Type Talk at Work, Otto Kroeger and Janet M.Thuesen (New York: Delacorte Press, Bantam Doubleday, Dell Publishing 1992).

I'm not Crazy, I'm Just Not You, Roger R. Pearman and Sarah C. Albritton (Davies Black Publishing 1997).

RELATIONSHIP BOOKS

Anatomy of Love, Helen Fisher Ph.D. (Fawcett Columbine 1992).

You're Not What I Expected, Polly Young-Eisendrath Ph.D (Fromm International Publishing 1993).

365 Reflections on Marriage, Eva Shaw (Adams Media 1999).

16 Ways to Love your Lover, Otto Kroeger and Janet M. Thuesen.

(New York: Delacorte Press, Bantam Doubleday, Dell Publishing 1994).

You Are Not My Type, Paul D. Tieger and Barbara Barron-Tieger (Canada: Little Brown & Co. 2000).

How to Stay Lovers for Life, Sharyn Wolf (Penguin Putnam, Inc, 1998).

The Nine Types of Lovers, Daphne Rose Kingma (Conari Press 1999).

The Eight Essential traits of Couples Who Thrive, Susan Page (Dell Publishing 1994).

COMMUNICATION MALE/FEMALE

That's Not What I Meant, Deborah Tannen Ph.D. (Ballantine Books 1986).

You Just Don't Understand, Deborah Tannen Ph.D. (Ballantine Books 1990).

Index

Abstract, 24–5
Active Listening, 133
Actualizing Soulmate, 24, 40
Adapting your Style, 135–9
Advocating Soulmate, 24, 40
Aggressive Communication, 151
Analyzing, 21, 24, 31–2, 34, 37–40, 63–4, 90, 113–14, 139, 166, 191–204
Artisan (see Playmate)
Assertive Communication, 150, 152
Attachment (see Relating)

Body Language, 129–32
Brainstorming, 21, 23, 24, 26–7, 61–2, 89, 112–13, 139, 165, 191–204

Closed Questions, 132–33
Communication Process, 47, 121–32, 137–8
Concrete, 21, 24–5
Conflict Resolution, 153–6
Conscious Competence/Incompetence, 2

Dating Game, 76–96
Dating Stage, xii, 76–7
Dating Rituals, 83–4, 92
Decision Making, 29–31, 160–3
Decision-Making Functions, 24, 31–4, 37, 62–5
Delivery, 128–31
Dialogue, 124, 125–32
Direction of Energy, 35–6, 66, 191–204
Distracting Factors, 78–9

Empathy Statements, 157–9
Experiencing, 21, 23, 24, 26–7, 37, 60–1, 88, 112, 139, 165, 191–204
Exploring Options (In Decision Making), 159–63, 168–9
Extroverting or Extraverting (see Direction of Energy)

Extroverting Actualizer, 38, 201
Extroverting Advocate, 38, 202–3
Extroverting Improvizer, 37, 192
Extroverting Innovator, 38, 199
Extroverting Manoeverer, 37, 191
Extroverting Marshaller, 38, 197
Extroverting Nurturer, 37, 194
Extroverting Regulator, 37, 196

Factors of Attraction, 77
Feedback, 30, 140–3
Feeling Preference, 29–31
Female/Male Differences (see Male/Female Differences)
Flirtation Signs and Signals, 80–2
Functions, 20–44, 59–62, 66, 71, 73, 88–91, 112–14, 138–9, 164–6

Gender Differences (see Male/Female Differences)
Generous Listening, 155–6
Goals, 101–8, 116
Guardians (see Helpmate)
Guiding Principles, 105–7, 118–19

Harmonizing, 21, 23, 31, 33, 34, 37–40, 63–5, 90, 114, 139, 166, 191–204
Helpmate, 4, 7, 8, 12–13, 16–18, 24–6, 30–1, 37–40, 53–9, 86, 111, 126–7, 129, 131, 137, 164, 191–204
Holidays, 183–4, 187

Idealist (see Soulmate)
Improvizing Playmate, 24, 37–40
Information Gathering Functions, 21, 23–9, 37, 60–2, 65–6
Innovating Mindmate, 24, 40
Interactive Activities, 178
Interests (Shared), 159
Introverting (see Direction of Energy)

Introverting Actualizer, 38, 201–2
Introverting Advocate, 38, 203–4
Introverting Improvizer, 37, 193–4
Introverting Innovator, 38, 200
Introverting Manoeverer, 37, 192
Introverting Marshaller, 38, 194
Introverting Nurturer, 37, 194
Introverting Regulator, 37, 197
Intuiting (see Abstract)

Languages of Lovemates, 126–8
Leisure Time, 177–9, 185–7
Lifeline, 68–9
Limerance (see Dating)
Lovemaps, 79–80
Lovemate, 1–19, 20–1, 24, 37–40, 52, 59, 71, 85–8, 110–12, 163–4, 173
Loving Styles, 20–44, 77, 110–12, 163–4, 191–204
Lust (see Dating)

Male/Female Differences, 49–51, 65–6, 70, 134, 181–3
Managing Reality, 108–9
Manoeuvring Playmate, 24, 37–40
Mapping your Relationship, 65–75
Mating Stage, xii, 97–120
Marshalling Mindmate, 24, 40
Mindmate, 4, 7, 9, 13–14, 16–18, 24–6, 30–1, 37–40, 53–9, 87, 111, 126–7, 129, 131, 137–8, 164, 191–204

Nature, 45–6
Nurture, 45–6
Nurturing Helpmate, 24, 37–40

Open-ended Questions, 132

PAUSE technique, 153–6
Paraphrasing, 134–5
Passive Activities, 178–9
Playing Field, 84–5
Playmate, 4, 7, 8, 10–11, 16–18, 24–6, 30–1, 37–40, 53–9, 86, 110, 126–7, 129, 131, 137, 164, 191–204

Positions, 152-5
Prioritizing, 174–7, 185
Profiling the Relationship (see Mapping the Relationship)

Quality Time, 171–89

Rational (see Mindmate)
Recalling, 21, 23, 24, 26–7, 37, 60–2, 88, 112, 139, 165, 191–204
Receiving the Message, 124
Regulating Helpmate, 24, 37–40
Relating Stage, xii, 121–147

Self Assessment: Functions, 32–4
Self Assessment: Temperament, 5–8
Sensing (see Concrete)
Sending the Message, 124, 125–31
Separate Activities, 179
Shared Interests, 159
Soulmate, 4, 5, 7, 9, 15–18, 16–18, 24–6, 30–1, 37–40, 53–9, 87, 111, 126–7, 129, 131, 138, 164, 191–204
Sources of Conflict, 148–50
Submissive Communication, 151–2
Systematizing, 21, 23, 24, 31–2, 34, 37–40, 63–4, 90, 113, 139, 165–6, 191–204

Tasks, 104
Temperament, 2–10, 24, 37–40, 41, 45, 55–9, 65–6, 72, 136–7, 180–1, 191–204
Thinking Preference, 29–31
TO FOCUS Personality Lenses, 46–9

Unconscious Competence/Incompetence, 2
Unique Situation Lens, 47, 65–6, 67–8

Values, 105–7, 117–18
Valuing, 21, 23, 24, 31, 33, 34, 37–40, 63–5, 71–2, 91, 114, 139, 166, 191–204
Vision Statements, 99–101, 117
Visioning, 21, 23, 24, 26, 28, 61–2, 89, 113, 139, 165, 191–204

Word Choice, 93, 124, 125-8